Pour !

en souhaitant que ce livre
puisse apporter quelque assistance
à son travail et à sa vie
en reconnaissance de l'aide
qu'elle m'a apportée
pour l'éditer
Avec gratitude
Luce Irigaray

Paris, le 14 janvier 2020

Luce Irigaray

Sharing the Fire

Outline of a Dialectics of Sensitivity

palgrave
macmillan

Luce Irigaray
Paris, France

ISBN 978-3-030-28329-2   ISBN 978-3-030-28330-8   (eBook)
https://doi.org/10.1007/978-3-030-28330-8

Cover illustration: Maram_shutterstock.com

This Palgrave Macmillan imprint is published by the registered company Springer Nature Switzerland AG
The registered company address is: Gewerbestrasse 11, 6330 Cham, Switzerland

For you for me

This outline of a dialectics of sensitivity
born of an amorous desire
in search of its becoming incarnate
in us, between us, and in the world

Contents

1

Hypothesis: Longing for Another Absolute Than Knowledge

Is humanity coming to an end or merely reaching a stage which calls for a radical cultural evolution? This cannot happen through a blindly forging ahead but, rather, through a return to that which can still grant us a rebirth, a development and a flowering that we have neglected until now. In an age in which we are recapitulating and interpreting our history, it would be appropriate to question our way of conceiving of human being itself, the one who is in great part the cause of this history. It could be useful to wonder about what could be the truth of a human being. Does not our conception of the latter appear today as a sort of hypothesis which has supported a cultural construction which is henceforth deeply shaken? Does the subjectivity which underpinned our culture correspond with our real being? And does the objective absolute, to which the human being supposedly longed, fit its real aspirations? If this were the case, why ought our being be kept split in various parts? Is not such a split a symptom of the necessity of pursuing our development in a way which permits our unification?

It seems that the privilege attached to our mental aptitude(s) has been the result of the difficult task of acquiring standing up and gaining mastery of our surroundings in order to satisfy our various needs. To succeed in that,

© The Author(s) 2019
L. Irigaray, *Sharing the Fire*,
https://doi.org/10.1007/978-3-030-28330-8_1

man has used his additional neurons to the detriment of the cultivation of his physical and sensitive belonging. However, these neurons need energy for functioning, and this energy begins to be lacking. For want of having taken into account the link between his body and his mind, man has become an organism which can no longer function. He looks like a robot which demands an external source of energy for working. Hence his dependence on external energy reserves and the diverse conflicts which arise from that. Hence also the fatal illnesses with which man is today confronted. In reality, man becomes more and more weak, and the countless techniques to which he resorts cannot compensate for his lack of natural energy.

We must thus wonder about the means of recovering the source of our original energy and of cultivating it. We may note that our culture until now has been determined by our needs, including those for supra-sensitive ideals, transcendent beings and moral rules. Perhaps the way of evolving would be to build henceforth culture starting from our desire(s). What is more, do we not need desire as the new basis for an individual and collective culture? Indeed, desire can answer our current lack of energy and the necessity of gathering ourselves together again. Obviously it is then a matter of our desire between living beings, especially between humans, and not of our desire for objects, be they even spiritual ones.

Sharing desire and love with the other(s) and intending to care in this way about the future of nature and humanity might look a little ingenuous. However, is it not a means to recover a source of energy and to cultivate our longing for the absolute without this becoming somehow or other destructive or nihilistic? Is not aiming at the absolute through my desire for the other an opportunity to approach, in a dialectical manner, my aspiration after the absolute without cutting it off from a natural rooting? And also a way of acknowledging that this relation is the origin and the end of a human becoming which must be of my own in order to be shared?

Surprisingly philosophers and moralists, quoting only them, leap over a stage in their view on human becoming—that of the cultivation of our sensitive and sensuous life. They talk about moral duties regarding social or political coexistence but say very little about the desire to be in communion with the other(s), which ought to be the most original link we ought to experience and cultivate towards a common life.

Desire is what allows us to gather ourselves together and gather together with the other(s). But this gathering together does not happen through moral imperatives or supra-sensitive ideals, but through that which compels us to collect ourselves and collect with the other(s). Desire grants us the opportunity to both unify ourselves and unite with the other(s) by what concerns us. It does not impose on us splitting ourselves into various parts, beginning with body, soul and spirit with their respective needs and duties. Desire appeals to our whole being, what is more putting it in touch with itself, with the other(s) and with the world. Desire brings us close to us, to the other, to the world. And such proximity remains linked with our natural belonging while longing for the absolute. Desire aspires after connecting, in us and between us, nature with the most sublime fulfilment.

Desire arises from the void opened in us by taking our difference from the other into account. It contributes to our holding in ourselves, to unifying our self from what is particular to us, but also to longing for the other as the one who is needed for us to become ourselves.

While being faithful to that which is in the beginning, desire endlessly aims at its fulfillment because the absolute after which it aspires can never be completely reached. Desire also connects the most intimate with the most remote. And yet, desire does not overcome opposites, it does not know them. Perhaps contradiction has no sense for it and results from its ignorance, its repression, its being reduced to instinct and drive, or to an abstract energy already cut off from its natural source. Life knows an absolute without opposites and contradiction, something to which the character of Antigone, for example, bears witness. But this absolute requires us to respect difference(s) and each to be faithful to its particularity.

Longing for the absolute takes root in our longing for life. Such longing must evolve in accordance with our own development but it cannot relinquish its natural rooting. That which allows this to happen is the love of the other, a love which is both love for the other and love from the other, and thus presupposes a reciprocity which precedes any moral imperative, and even any conscious decision. Such a love is not separable from desire—as said about Eros by Phaedrus in the *Symposium* of Plato. And desire also needs it to be reciprocal in order to be really human and able to keep its relation to transcendence and its potential—which is impossible without it being somehow or other equipotential.

Desire acts as a bridge between soma, soul and spirit. It allows our physical matter to be transformed without remaining subjected to a mere natural alternative between growing and decreasing. Desire opens a transcendental horizon, in a simply natural motion, through relating to the other as naturally different. Beyond the fact that desire animates our body with an energy which exceeds vitality and survival, it also increases this energy by communing with another living energy. And the transcendental horizon, which is opened by the respect for another living being as different, permits us to modify the nature of our energy and of our matter itself. Such a process makes us capable of overcoming our subjection to nature while being faithful to it.

In this way we can escape the alternative between growth and decline without having for all that to keep in abeyance our evolution through supra-sensitive ideals. Then we enter another economy and another logic which do not neglect the properties of life and the margin of freedom that a human being has to preserve and cultivate.

Desire is also a means that is granted us to overcome past metaphysics while acknowledging its merits. Longing for the other as a path towards the absolute means that we long for more than being(s)—we long for an incarnate transcendence. And this allows us to surmount some of the main dichotomies at work in our traditional Western philosophy: for example, existence-essence; nature-spirit; sensitivity-conceptuality; being-Being. If desire is that which determines our being present to ourselves, to the world, to the other(s), then most of the dichotomies which supported our past logic lose their usefulness and even their meaning. Indeed, our physical matter is already subjective, and not merely objective, thanks to the desire which animates it; our sexuate identity, which sometimes could appear as an essence, is a crucial element of our existence; sensitive or sensuous attraction for the other, different from us by nature, is a longing for transcendence to quote some of them. Even the opposition between being and becoming is then obsolete, because we cannot be without continuing to carry out our development, notably through relating to the other as transcendent to ourselves.

The contribution of desire to our being, our becoming, and our relating to the world and to the other(s) has not been taken enough into account by our past culture. Desire has too often been considered to be a mere instinct or drive and not the bridge between body and spirit, immanence and transcendence, materiality and spirituality that it represents, above all as a desire for the other as different from us by nature. What is more, the dynamism provided by desire has generally been used without being recognized as such. There is no doubt, for example, that desire is that which maintains the motion towards the absolute in the Hegelian dialectics. And yet, he does not think a lot about the nature of desire, about its true relation to the absolute and its intervention in what he considers to be the absolute of an objectivity corresponding with our subjectivity. And this perpetuates a blindness regarding the truth and the ethics which are necessary for ensuring a possible becoming for ourselves and for the whole world.

For a long time, one of my projects has been to write a book on each of the main elements which constitute the matter of the world and of all the living beings. My book on Nietzsche (*Marine Lover*) tackles the question of water and my book on Heidegger (*The Forgetting of Air*) the question of air. *Elemental Passions* and *Through Vegetal Being* have to deal with our relation to earth. I wondered how to broach the question of fire. At first, I imagined doing that through Marx and the problem of human work in the production of goods. More recently, it became obvious to me that fire concerns above all desire and the way through which our human being can develop beyond a merely natural growth. Desire acts as the sap and the dynamism that we have to acknowledge and cultivate to make blossom and share our human being. Desire is our internal fire, our internal sun. Our tradition has underestimated, and even ignored, the importance of desire for our human accomplishment. It is the case in the Hegelian dialectics, which leaps too quickly from matter to light without lingering enough on the role of desire to pass from our physical to our spiritual belonging. Hegel neglects to consider the necessity of the fire of desire in the transformation of matter, beginning with our own, and of the dialectical motion that such a process and its sharing require.

2

The Desire to Be

Giving Birth to Our to Be

Letting happen the ones who we are does not only mean letting our being appear but allowing our 'to be'[1] to exist, opening a place in which it can take place and enter into presence. It is to give back our 'to be' to

---

[1] I apologize for the quite inelegant use of 'to be', and this from the very beginning of the volume. However, to use 'being'—or even 'Being'—instead of 'to be' makes the meaning that I try to convey incomprehensible. Indeed, being is a present participle, which expresses a current modality or way of existing of a/our 'to be', or a substantive which amounts to a fixation of this modality or existence in a noun which is presumed to indicate its essence. And yet, if 'to be' can become incarnate in the present, this incarnation never corresponds to its comprehensive potential. Nevertheless, far from reducing 'to be' to an idea or a cultural essence, I rather intend to send this/our 'to be' back to a natural origin. I might dare say that I attempt to give it back to its natural essence—as an oak designates the natural essence of a particular tree, and a man or a woman designates the natural essence of a human being. My use of 'to be' is thus a call for a return to a real living potential and not for a subjection to an ideal essence. It also means that every existence must be rooted in a unity from which it arouses and to which it must be able to return so as to not risk ending in nothing. In our Western languages, in particular in English, it is difficult to make clear such a meaning that the verb 'être' in French or 'Sein' in German can more easily express. So, for example, 'être' can signify both the singularity of a being, especially of a living being, and its comprehensive potential and dynamism. I thus allow myself to, sometimes, use 'to be', instead of the usual 'being' or 'Being', whatever the inconvenience in reading, because I hope that this will contribute to a better perception of the thinking that I try to pass on.

© The Author(s) 2019
L. Irigaray, *Sharing the Fire*,
https://doi.org/10.1007/978-3-030-28330-8_2

7

life. This cannot amount to merely inciting it to become apparent but rather asks us to gather our selves together, to be in communion with ourselves in order to remember the 'to be' that we are and to ensure a collecting of our selves starting from which this 'to be' may become present—also to the other. To be present to one another requires us to let our 'to be' be present in each—as a question, a mystery, a life of which we must take care and bring into the world.

Opening out to an encounter with an other is opening up to a meeting between two 'there is' in search of their 'to be': firstly as 'he is' or 'she is'. The neuter would represent an embodiment of being which can give birth to our 'to be' through the event of a meeting between two desires from which a spark flies out which questions us about our being. The neuter would be an inauthentic stage of being which can give rise to the advent of our 'to be'.

If the end of our past metaphysics can happen thanks to an advent, this of the disclosure of the truth corresponding to our 'to be' perhaps grants us the chance of entering into a new universal and transhistorical epoch. Indeed, history and the particularities of being that are embodied in it are only partial, unconscious, thus alienating and preventing the unveiling and entering into presence of our 'to be'. Wondering about this/our 'to be' as such is probably the task which is incumbent on us in our epoch. What can contribute towards its achievement is, no doubt, to interpret the withdrawal of 'to be' from past metaphysics, to which Heidegger points, but also to consider the part of this 'to be' that metaphysics did not take into account, especially regarding the relationship between us as subjects who are naturally different. The philosophers who criticize our past philosophical tradition do not wonder whether the elusive character of 'to be', and even its forgetting, do not result from our neglecting what occurs between us, notably as sexually different. And they do not imagine that it is there that the question concerning 'to be' must be asked and something of the enigma of this 'to be' has to be both unveiled and kept.

The advent of our 'to be' perhaps happens in a meeting between us. What is then unveiled is also veiled again, notably because of the faithfulness to the ontological destiny specific to each which makes our meeting possible. This unveiling and veiling again is the place where 'to be' comes into the world and withdraws from the world for those who meet together, but more generally for the world itself.

In reality this unveiling, like this veiling, is triple: with regard to ourselves, to the other and to the event of the meeting and what it incarnates. The advent of 'to be' cannot stop with any being, it must remain constantly happening. However, such a happening cannot amount to a projection forward of its potential or to our wandering outside of ourselves; instead, it must correspond to a moving towards reaching our 'to be', towards the place of a repose from which we can develop and which represents a stasis in our growing. Such repose and development are both particular and shared. They need a co-belonging of the two components of humanity who desire to find a restful stasis in a union with one another, a union which cannot last. And yet, they cannot find repose only in themselves either, because they long for one another and for uniting with one another. But there where 'to be' happens, between them, they cannot dwell. Hence an infinite quest, which sometimes aspires after being kept in abeyance in the beyond as the place of a possible stasis. However, giving up the quest amounts to giving up any 'to be'.

To be corresponds to an advent which sometimes occurs in a union between two living beings, especially two different incarnations of human being. Each of them longs for their 'to be', a 'to be' to which they give birth without being truly able to live it, even if their desire to be determines the horizon in which they try to stay, an horizon woven from a tension between two beings, the one that they originally are and the one at which they aim as an achievement from their origin. Desire is that which maintains our striving to forge links between the two. Desire must arise from our origin and open up to the infinite thanks to the finiteness of the ones who desire. Our sexuation is that which enables us to maintain our striving for opening up to the infinite in space and time from our finiteness.

Our sexuate determination can also allow us to combine natural belonging and cultural development. But culture then must take into account our natural belonging. We have to shape ourselves in order that our own nature should develop as such and appear through disclosing what or who it is. Thus substituting idea(s) for flowering, or the fabrication of ourselves as a cultural product for the cultivation of our natural belonging, must be abandoned to carry out the work of moulding our nature so that it should become really human and our life should turn into a human incarnation in faithfulness to its original determinations.

Our impulse to create must be in harmony with the impulse of life itself and we must discover mediations which permit us to become fully human while remaining alive and preserving the immediacy of a living dynamism, in particular thanks to our sexuate desire. It is such a desire which brings energy, determination(s) and limit(s) to our being, and thus makes our spirit able to develop without cutting us off from our nature. It is such a desire which allows our nature to tell itself, to unite the matter of our body with words, in a way our physical element with our meta-physical element, and a natural language with a language of thought ('Temps et être/'Time and Being', Heidegger 1976: pp. 88–89/pp. 50–51).

Natural language arises above all from a desire which remains rooted in our body, but most generally from a vision of the world, which provides the language of thinking with a specific syntax. Our sexuate body acts as a sort of framework which imprints its structure on our saying. Thus patterns, especially linguistic patterns, are not merely imposed from an outside, transforming in this way human being into a sort of automaton, they are supplied by our living nature itself. Our sexuate body operates as what enables us to overcome the split between matter and form—it produces matter with form, and form with matter. It acts as a living intermediary which allows us to develop without a frame which is technically conceived and imposed—Heidegger would say a *Gestell*. Perhaps I could also suggest that it is the place which leads us to pass from immanence to transcendence, from an ontical to an ontological level—but also from the one to the other.

Dwelling Place Opened by Desire

Our desire questions us about the space and places already existing. It crosses them, makes its way through them towards a potential clearing. It is a call for leaving our past enclosures and confinements, and opens new places in which to dwell. It spaces the space already structured and inhabited. It invites us to enter another abode here and now without having to go abroad to discover this opportunity.

The other as other provides us with a new perspective on the place in which we stay, a place determined by our natural belonging and environment but also by our sociocultural background. The attraction for the other is the first trajectory, the first trail starting from which the possible existence of another world can be sensed, a world in which we would like to live. If the other reciprocates the track that my desire drew, this already supplies a double reference to outline the horizon of a place in which desire can become incarnate. Withdrawing into ourselves furnishes other coordinates towards a spatial architecture, above all if a double withdrawal exists, our own and that of the other, but also our respective coming and going from the outside to the inside of ourselves. In this architecture, our sensory perceptions and our gestures also sketch points, lines, surfaces which contribute to building another space within the space in which we were situated, a place that desire clears, opening to and little by little creating another world.

In order that we should dwell in such a world, a spatial volume is necessary. It is the part of ourselves which is the most extraneous to the voluminous one which enables us to open this space: our sexuate belonging. It makes us capable of building a volume from the void that is opened in each of us, and also between us, by acknowledging that we are not the other, that we are not, and never will be, the whole of the human being. Agreeing to take on this negative, in other words to assume our particularity, we create a void which does not correspond to a lack but to that which allows us to shape a place of our own thanks to which we can open up to the other without relinquishing ourselves. It needs such a void to take place in us, and between us, in order that we should permit the other to appear as other and our presence to one another to happen.

Desire reopens the place which was allocated to us by the world into which we came. This world is not truly ours and we must in a way free ourselves from it in order to discover the place which is suitable for us. We must un-shelter ourselves to sense and build the place which can really shelter us. Desire which reopens the world into which we came by birth must also open places in which it can spread out and make room for a repose from which we can develop ourselves.

Desire, which compels us to gather ourselves together, while leaving a world which was not truly our own, must also build a place in which we can commune with ourselves. It must arise from the void which is opened by our assuming our particularity and arrange a place in which we can take shelter while giving rise to a coexistence with an other who is different from us by nature.

To be presupposes to dwell. Besides, the two words have the same Indo-European etymology: 'bhû' or 'bheu', which remains the root of words in certain languages—for example, the German 'bin', 'bist', 'bis' have clearly the same root 'bhû' as 'bauen' (*L'introduction à la métaphysique*, pp. 80–83; *Introduction to Metaphysics*, pp. 74–78, Heidegger 1967a). To dwell cannot confine itself to living on earth as a mortal—as Heidegger asserts (in particular in 'Bâtir, Habiter, Penser'/'Building, Dwelling, Thinking'; Heidegger 1958b, 1993)—which amounts to determining our being and dwelling mainly from an outside, in particular from the world in which we are situated. In order that we should be what first matters is to inhabit our own body. Our sexuate belonging allows us to do that through the morphology and the relational limits with which it provides us. This belonging in a way corresponds to a nothing of flesh which gives us our own flesh and allows our body to take place.

Thanks to our sexuate belonging we can dwell in our body, we can be our body and even enter into relation with another body. Our sexuation enables us to lay out a room which favours the relationships with the other as a natural being. However, these sorts of relations are not the same as those that our sociocultural background has in store for us— they open a new place in the common space. The traditional distinction between private life and public life probably has such significance, the former keeping the linguistic forms of 'building' faithful to the Indo-European root 'bhû', which means that to be presupposes to dwell.

In what is called a private house, to dwell ought to have as its first aim the preservation and cultivation of life. The home is supposed to shelter such cultivation, to preserve a place within which life can develop while being protected. In this place, each—and firstly the couple who open this space by mutual desire—ought to watch over being possible for the other to dwell in him or herself. That which permits a cultivation of our living beings is then our cohabiting, that is, our sharing a place that is built in accordance with our relational requirements as living beings and in which their cultivation can develop thanks to a mutual concern. Surrounded by the space of the home, such a care also requires each to wrap the body and the words of the other with a space specific to him or to her. Each must both help the other to free him or herself from what cuts them off from their own 'to be', so preventing them from returning to it, and be careful about cultivating this 'to be' by wrapping around them a space which allows them to be faithful to themselves and their becoming. This mutual care is neither a mere abnegation nor a love extraneous to desire, including an erotic desire and its sharing. It is what builds the place in which a carnal union can occur as a way to fulfil our own 'to be'. Dwelling in a place, a home, which is so doubly safeguarded, might bring or restore to us the unity of our being, a unity that the relational properties of our natural belonging already grant us.

Such a belonging requires us to respect, but also to build, bridges between the other and ourselves—which means considering and cultivating our desire. It is desire which, while attracting us to one another, collects the one and the other in their own place. If desire clears a passage to the other, it also contributes towards bringing us into the presence of ourselves and of one another. Desire liberates us from the fetters of imposed requirements, habits and limitations, which kept us trapped, and it invites us to appear in accordance with our own limits.

Moreover, because of the non-being that the respect for the difference of the other asks us to assume, desire restores us to the integrity of a not yet being freed from the fetters of past being(s). It also reminds us that any pre-given symbolical requirement has to direct our meeting, apart from that of acknowledging that we correspond only to a component of the symbol that human being represents. It is our conjunction—which does not mean our complementarity—which constitutes this symbol, and it is from such a conjunction that a symbolical order can arise. As humans, we lack roots of our own, and incarnating our union is that which can provide us with a place suitable for our dwelling.

We then enter a space which no longer obeys the system of measurements to which we were accustomed. Expanses, distances, intervals and so on exist, or at least ought to exist, but they are not measurable in a way external to them, nor, what is more, by universal and constant mensurations. Expanses, distances, intervals where we are placed and which exist between us are created by our being in relation, and they change continually. Hence the challenge that the relationship between us represents. It reopens the space allotted to us by our historical and sociocultural belonging and opens up to another space for which estimations are yet lacking. We must build this space and build it together, at least in part.

The Gift of Nothing

Fortunately, by freeing ourselves from the way of inhabiting the world to which we were accustomed, we reopen a space which allows us to return to live in nature as macro- and microcosm. Liberated from an exile partly constructed against our real being, we are given back to our natural belonging—which implies a certain manner of dwelling determined by the place that our body represents, notably through its sexuation. Indeed, a merely physical, and supposedly in the neuter belonging, does not provide us with a dwelling apart from one artificially structured and imposed on us. But we, then, no longer inhabit ourselves and we coexist in a space–time which is historically assessed according to the sciences and the techniques of one epoch only. They are thus predetermined and they are shaped by us more than they allow us to dwell— they attract us outside of us, in search of us, but we do not find in this way a closeness to ourselves again. We are subjected to a device extraneous to our flesh living at present, a device which cuts us off from any self-affection.

Only the flesh of the other, as a flesh present to us, can give us back our self-affection. Self-affection of the other can bring us back to our own self-affection in particular through touch, because in this touch a call of the other already lies. As such it reminds us of the properties of life, in particular of its link with the other. However, if we have not opened in ourselves the void space that the respect for the difference of the other involves, we do not perceive all that their touch tells to us.

We are affected, but we can identify neither the other nor ourselves in such a feeling reduced to the neutrality of a 'there is', which does not enable us to distinguish an 'it is me' from an 'it is you'. We are thus not capable of recognizing what is perceived as relating to us, to the other or to the union between us. We lack the aptitude for staying in ourselves while perceiving the signs of the presence of the other. To succeed in doing that, we must maintain in ourselves a void, a virgin space thanks to which we gather ourselves together so that we could preserve our own being and be able to welcome the other as other. Acknowledging and being faithful to our sexuate belonging allows us to act in this way. In reality, this belonging is nothing material as such but it gives rise to physical forms. Instead of wondering about these forms, we reduce them either to matter or to abstract forms, unless we use them as a mere tool. Yet we could consider them to be the flowering of our life in its particularity before any division into matter and form(s)—they are a presence of the life in which we become incarnate and manifest the ones who we are, also to the other. They are the shapes thanks to which we can collect ourselves and welcome one another as living beings in the transcendent subjective materiality of our flesh. Our sexuate exchanges ought to take place, including at a carnal level, within the horizon of such transcendence.

By taking on the void created by our difference in order to respect such transcendence, we overcome nihilism, notably by acknowledging the positive value of the nothing itself, instead of letting it become a nothingness which undermines our whole existence. The negative or the void, which entailed the transformation of the truth of beings into essences, through which our becoming had been put on hold, is now assumed as a nothing which ought to originally be a driving force in the evolution of this becoming.

Such a nothing also contributes towards maintaining a place for our gathering ourselves together. Because we are able to take on the nothing, we can also open ourselves up to the other without losing ourselves. We have gathered ourselves together from a nothing of being which allows us to collect together the being that we are so that we could enter into presence of the other as other. The nothing of being grants us an internal horizon thanks to which we can gain an access to our being as such.

It is because I am not you—more generally not else—that I can commune both with me and with you. Gathering myself together enables me to gather together with the other. The distance from me, that taking on a non-being creates, makes it possible for me to be close both to myself and to the other through assuming our difference. Distancing me from myself and from the other permits a getting closer without a lack of differentiation, without a confusion or a fusion. Closeness can happen without us being reduced to a juxtaposition, an enumeration, a sum of unities presumed to be the same ones and between which proximity and distance amount to an accounting assessment either. In order that closeness to one another should occur, we must be one another, one for the other, the guardians of the non-being that we are.

This not-being, in a way this void in being, does not contain anything of its own, unlike the thing on which Heidegger comments (cf. 'La chose'/'The Thing', Heidegger 1958a). It only shelters while preserving; that is, it allows the non-being that we are to welcome the being of the other without appropriating it—we can thus give him or her back to it. We even can grant them the perception of what is nothing, the highest gift that we can offer to one another. Such a gift is that which permits us to gather ourselves together while relating to and with the other living and even not living beings, also with consideration for temporality. It prepares us for the happening of a not yet, and gives us back a viewpoint on history—our own but also that in which we took place. The void which is opened by assuming our non-being is what enables us to dwell by dwelling in ourselves and co-existing with the other. To appropriate the other, making the other our own by nullifying its otherness, amounts to breaking into this void and destroying the possibility that the other might be welcome in it, but also to annihilating our own possibility of dwelling, because dwelling needs the capability of staying in oneself. To appropriate someone or something, instead of being appropriate to ourselves, is that which calls into question our human dwelling and the shelter of the not-being that it requires.

Besides, appropriating the other is possible only through its annihilation. Indeed, the other as other cannot stand simply before us as an object, be it material or spiritual, which we could have at hand.

Such a hold could take place only as a sort of murder of the other, either by overtly killing him or her or, more indirectly, by depriving them of their breathing, of their life. Relating to and with the other needs our working out an interiority, which allows us to approach him or her while maintaining a material and spiritual distance from them. Entering into the presence of the other can occur only from a distance.

Obviously we can approach one another as belonging to a same already existing world, but such a proximity is not a real closeness, it is determined by other than us. What permits our closeness to one another to occur is desire, an appeal which is aroused in us and longs for uniting with the other. And this desire wants closeness but also distance which makes closeness possible.

It can happen that our desire gets lost in a set of reflections or images, notably of the other, which prevents closeness from being reached and shared. We must avoid these modes of approaching which amount to a refusal to venture to meet the other by giving up any subjection to sameness. Our desire must renounce any approach in which it does not take on a negative, a non-being, which it cannot overcome without running the risk of being itself reduced to nothing.

Assuming Non-being

Assuming our non-being creates a discontinuity in our way of experiencing time. Only a human subjectivity can live through such a discontinuity thanks to its memory and the expectation that desire maintains. The void corresponding to our non-being is the place in which remembrance and anticipation of the future can link together with respect for each other. And this allows us to enter into presence as different— taking on our non-being has opened a place where such a meeting can occur in the present against the background of a continuance, of which it does not tear the becoming, despite being ecstatic in relation to it. This requires a memory of our 'to be' and not only of some or other aspect of our being. Only the remembrance of a living being in its whole can contribute to a weaving of time which does not lead astray from the process of becoming. Only by considering this living being and considering ourselves against the background of the unity of our respective lives, can we link together in a lasting way alternations between being and non-being, in ourselves and between us.

The comments of Heidegger on the 'thing', as that which is capable of gathering, cannot completely apply to us as living beings (cf. 'La chose'/'The Thing', Heidegger 1958a). Whatever the properties of the 'jug', given as an example of thing, it is not truly living and cannot correspond with us while preserving our respective differences as a human is able to do. We can imagine that it acts in this way but it is then a matter of our projections: onto it in the present; about it at the time of its moulding; onto the memory of its use. This does not permit a weaving of time, especially with a jug, at least of a living time. Such a weaving can happen only when we are in relationship with another living being, with which we can really exchange, and we supply time with the space that it needs for its weaving. The fact that a jug can contain, thus also retain, something does not mean its ability to hold a relation to/with each other.

Sexuation is a structure of our being which allows us to gather ourselves as a whole and connect ourselves to one another without any making external to us—as is needed for a thing. This is possible thanks to the non-being and the void with which the specificity and the difference of our sexuate belonging provide us. Alas, the latter is too often used almost as a technique in order to produce pleasure, to release energy or to reproduce human species, which annihilates its power to produce ourselves and leads to 'the little death'—of which Freud speaks—or to the death of parents according to Hegel.

Why has the potential of our sexuate belonging not been acknowledged, notably as a poietic aptitude of nature itself, even though it can correspond to the four causes at the origin of production defined by Aristotle? If our culture has perceived that the vegetal being has in itself the ability to develop independently of any making up, it has not discovered that our sexuate belonging partly shares such an ability. Perhaps we could then suggest, in Aristotelian terms, that our soma is the material cause, our sexuation the formal cause, our desire the efficient cause, and that the final cause is not the reproduction of the human species but the accomplishment of our humanity, especially by our uniting with one another. Indeed, it is between us and thanks to our sexuate desire that we can disclose to one another something of our being through a perception of ourselves that we have to transform into the ones who we are. Unfortunately, we too often reduce our sexuate belonging to a tool in order to produce a being external to us—that is, to something that our past metaphysics was able to imagine—instead of considering it to be a path towards the blossoming of our being. We have not yet discovered either the way or the truth of this sort of production.

We do not bloom as a flower; blooming for us occurs also thanks to the other. It is the other who contributes towards an un-sheltering of our being which allows us to develop and appear as the ones who we are. However, the other has not to substitute for the becoming of our own being; he or she must not want to subject our flowering to their own making up. The other must help us to blossom without removing us from our natural resources. The other must bring us back to these resources and not take us away from them. And such a gesture leads him or her to return to themselves and to live what results for them from all that.

Human being needs the other for discovering and embodying its own truth, but such a disclosure and accomplishment cannot be the result of a making, in the sense of a fabrication. They require us to let life occur in each. In other words, becoming, for a human, necessitates a dialectical process between activity and passivity in which the other takes part. If each has to develop by itself, it is also incited to develop by and for the other. But this incentive must serve a growing of our own.

Distributing activity and passivity between man and woman has prevented the fulfilment of the one and the other from happening. This also led to the development of a culture in which man himself has been reduced to powerlessness against the exploitation of his energy for which our technical world today calls him. Wanting to be unilaterally active in the production of energy, especially in the sexuate relationship, man henceforth ends up in being a passive fund of energy, which is used for the functioning of a world in which his development can no longer happen as being due to him, as being the result of his own undertaking. He missed linking active with passive, and resorting to the middle voice as the way of preparing a place in which he can dwell and become thanks to his own energy and a coexistence with the other living beings.

The middle voice allows us to connect desire with pathos, sexuate belonging with soma. It supplies us with the stance that the attraction or the projection of desire needs as a measure in order for it to remain incarnate. Sensitivity then provides the impetus of desire with a regulation which inscribes the transcendence of longing in our flesh, where it finds an anchorage really different from that supplied by supra-sensitive ideals.

The work of incarnation can be carried out through the structure that our sexuation represents, a structure which has a share in our body itself, but transcends it as a mere soma, especially by calling for a union with a body which is different and transcendent to ours. Energy can thus be kept for the work of our becoming without being solely used in deeds external to ourselves. Energy is then of use to the development and blossoming of each thanks to a mutual cultivation of our natural belonging. It contributes to the generation of a humanity in which creation and generation take part in a sort of dialogue between the word, that desire is, and the body, between acting and feeling—in each of us and between us.

Balancing acting and feeling requires us to be capable of transcendence with respect to ourselves. Such transcendence can be revealed to us in relating to and with an other who is naturally different from us. This relation can also disclose the transcendental potential of our sexuate belonging and how sexuation, as a structure which is part of us, can contribute to revealing truth—our truth, this of our own being.

Such a frame cannot be simply appropriated by us even though it determines what is particular to us. It also gives to us a margin of freedom with regard to the immanence of our natural belonging, a freedom which is both immanent and transcendent in relation to our bodily existence. It is that which can join and sometimes overcome the ontico-ontological split that Heidegger defines as a specific feature of our traditional metaphysics.

Our sexuate structure in a way has no materiality, but it is inseparable from our physical belonging. Its manner of operating is not completely controllable, visible, representable. It forces us to take into account the non-unveilable part of ourselves in order to appear as the ones who we are. Moreover, this appearing is provoked by or with the other, on the condition that he or she respects the most intimate part of our truth as something which escapes from their mastery and making.

The other contributes towards our being revealed to ourselves if he or she agrees to the fact that what they disclose to us will remain hidden from them. If things are not going this way, our sexuate belonging might act as a technical device being of use to cause a consumption of the ones who we are instead of it contributing to giving rise to, developing and making blossom the ones who we are. Alas, our traditional way of conceiving of sexuality often corresponds to the first tendency. Sexual intercourse is then considered to be an opportunity to spend energy or, at best, to beget children, but not to disclose our being and to expose it towards its cultivation. In the first case, human being finds in sexuality a more or less technically elaborate means to exhaust itself as a fund or a reserve of being, whereas in the second case sexuality can unveil, and even arouse, resources of being that we can obtain only in this way, notably thanks to a return to the ecstasy that our origin represents and a sharing of energy with the other.

Sexuation as First Logos

Our sexual intercourse, more generally our sexuate relations, escapes the risk of being the occasion of an exploitation, which each runs in them, only if they correspond to a link between two transcendences which venture to unite the mystery that 'to be' means to each. Those who take part in such a union then assume the ecstasy with respect to their origin that their specific sexuation represents, an ecstasy the sense of which they perpetuate through their search for a conjunction with the sexually different other. This conjunction—or copula—brings them together towards a becoming of their being. Sexual intercourse, more generally sexuate relations, in this way avoids using up the structure, which our sexuation is, by a subjection and an exploitation of the resources of being that a human being has in its care and which it must cultivate, notably through its relationship with the other(s).

Unfortunately, more often than not our sexuation has been reduced to an implement, being the matter of increasing and releasing our energy or of reproducing the human species. And yet its first function ought to be to bring us together, and even to favour how to adjust us to one another as different. Instead of our respective sexuate belongings being of use so that the vigour of our desire should produce an energy that we spend or exhaust in other than what corresponds to its origin and aim, energy awoken by the attraction between us could be used to modify each and each other in order to favour the union in us and between us of the body and soul, of our drives and our spiritual aspirations, of nature and word. Transforming into beauty—in a way into a work of art—the immediacy of our impulses can thus contribute to disclosing what or who we are to each of us and to one another.

That which drove us to urgently spend energy then becomes the opportunity to restrain ourselves in order to let happen something of our being as a particular incarnation standing out against an undifferentiated flow of life. Such an incarnation, besides the fact that it preserves and maintains our energy alive, allows us to cultivate this energy towards its growing and its sharing at a higher level, and without it being altered. This leads us to little by little be revealed to ourselves and to one another. In other words, something of the mystery of our being is so disclosed.

Such a disclosure must contribute neither to exhausting our energy reserves nor to uprooting us from our natural belonging, but to developing and making blossom the ones who we are. It must permit us to preserve, instead of exploiting, what appears of us thanks to the attention and care brought by and to our living fleshes—which provides our being with a shelter different from the permanence of an idea or a word. It is to our carnal memory and our heart that the being of each is now entrusted in order to ensure its remembrance and its becoming. This calls for the one and the other to welcome, in the present, what or who they are, each providing the other with a dwelling and a fleshly mirror thanks to which he or she can gather with themselves or come into presence without taking the risk of being rigidified by forms or appearances extraneous to life, without risking dissipating in appearing a growth of life which only occurs in a secret way, either. The shelter that each brings to the other must respect their mystery and wrap him or her in a presence which remains mysterious too. Two beings, capable of an autonomous self-affection, then, give assistance to each other in their becoming, without intervening in the latter in a manner which leads them astray from their own development. For a moment, each proposes to the other a repose and even a fertilization, in its own flesh—an invaluable stage in pursuing a becoming.

Such a 'gathering pause', as Heidegger would say, is different from this that our traditional logos can ensure. Indeed, it does not impose on us any permanence, conformity or homogeneity. It makes room for a stasis in our evolution, which grants a repose where our being sometimes can lie, is gathered in the intimacy of a silent presence. It neither exposes nor tells itself save through an ability to gather itself together thanks to the welcome of another flesh. It is that which can shelter before any articulate language. It is the first logos through which our 'to be' can be perceived, can dwell in a gathering pause, before continuing its way amongst beings, a journey in which it may be embodied in a manner through which it could forget itself. The other, then, can bring our being back to itself, give back to it a presence, provided that this other can safeguard its 'to be' and preserve this 'to be' from freezing in words or images in which it risks being homogenized or homogenizing, so cutting itself off from any living and carnal presence. It is by being faithful to ourselves as a flesh irreducible to any other that we become able to shelter the being of the other while protecting our own from its own forgetting and getting lost.

So returning to the simplest, humblest and most innocent hug means probably returning to the place in which our being can find an origin again—be born or be born again. Indeed, we then go back to that which from the very beginning determined us but we neither perceived nor acknowledged as a determination or a mediation. It acted without our knowing although it intervened in a way in our self-consciousness; which is proved by the particular structuring of our discourses. Nevertheless, we did not know this mediation and we need another mediation, a mediation of mediation, in order to assume it.

This mediation of mediation can be provided by an other, who perceives our self, which we cannot immediately perceive by ourselves, or through the result of an analysis of our own productions, for example of our discourse. In this way we can recover an immediacy in the perception of our sensitive being without either mistaking it for what it perceives or forcing it to become insensitive.

Our flesh is neither in the neuter nor lacking in differentiation, especially because of its sexuation. The question is: how can we perceive it as such given that sexuation in a sense is nothing perceptible—at least it is the case in our tradition? And for perceiving it, we have to resort to another logos, another logic in which interaction between two naturally different subjects has a privileged role.

It is not only through the other, and in the other, that our sexuate belonging can be revealed—as Hegel asserts—but also by our desire, more generally our way of desiring; that is, by our manner of entering into relation, the energy and modes of which are proper to our sexuate belonging.

In order to keep its transcendental nature, our desire needs to project itself onto the beyond, a beyond that cannot remain in the neuter or lacking in differentiation. It must correspond with the nature of our desire itself. However, this cannot be fulfilled without the existence of a difference which calls each beyond itself. This difference can neither act without individualizing nor be a mere quantitative one. Desire which aspires after the beyond, also aspires after the absolute, an absolute that it experiences as being truly its own. And yet, such a perception can occur only if we long for the other as a way to fulfil our flesh without losing our longing for the beyond.

Only a sexuate desire can achieve the paradox of becoming incarnate thanks to the other through a sort of dialectical process between finite and infinite, taking place between our longing for the beyond and our experiencing this one in ourselves. Our aspiration after the beyond must long for another living human being, who maintains its longing for an absolute from which its particular origin exiled it.

As it cannot become incarnate only from such an ec-stasis regarding its conception, a human being can reach its incarnation by taking charge of the task that desire drives it to carry out. In this way, it can overcome the feeling of its orphan and powerless finiteness through an experience of the infinite which permits its longing for the absolute to be incarnate in finiteness, an absolute always in becoming. Indeed, experiencing oneself as the source of the absolute can abolish time—can change it into eternity, Nietzsche perhaps would say—but not in a permanent way.

Infinity Arising from Finiteness

Desire has another function regarding the absolute in its connection with the relative. In reality, desire always wants the absolute, and it meets with disappointment when it becomes attached to some or other object, that is, to the relative. Desire is never aspiring after something, or even after someone reduced to an object. Desire wants desire, as a longing for the absolute is inherent to human being.

In a way, the same goes for desire as for consciousness according to Hegel. Is not consciousness, for Hegel, in search of self-consciousness as an absolute and not of the consciousness of some or other thing, reality, being and so on? An accomplished self-consciousness would correspond to an embodiment of the absolute of which subjectivity is in search, an absolute which would have been concealed by the attachment to some or other object or truth. But the other is never some or other one, and I cannot reduce him or her to such a relative reality after which either my desire or my consciousness would aspire. As such the other is the absolute of which I am in search, on the condition that he or she does not resign themselves to being some or other one, not to say some or other thing, for my desire or my consciousness. Escaping such a reduction, the other forces me to modify the surge which drives me towards them, to pursue my becoming by transforming my longing for the beyond. I could say that the other, then, absolves me from seizing him or her as a relative reality, be it appetitive or cognitive, by giving me back to the absolute of which I am in search—a thing that can be carried out only if the other keeps its radical qualitative otherness. Far from hindering my desire, such irreducible difference is that which maintains it alive.

As such, desire, better than knowledge, preserves our relation to the absolute. The other, if it succeeds in protecting its particularity thanks to self-affection, escapes from any knowledge of it. Whilst knowledge aims at appropriating, desire wants non-appropriation because this frees it from relativity.

Besides, desire is never a mere self-desire, as can be the case for consciousness. Desire is always also desire for the other, this other being not only the end but also the origin of desire. Desire never arises merely from the self, the other already plays a part in its springing up.

If consciousness is essentially egoistic, the same cannot apply to desire. Certainly, it is determined by our self, and this must know itself as desiring in order to be really able to desire. And yet, desire for the self cannot content itself with such relativity in its aspiration after the absolute. Desire does not aspire merely after the self and, furthermore, the self who desires is not merely one self. As well originally as in the present, the other intervenes in our desire, an other who cannot truly present itself or be represented but supports, also by this very fact, our longing for the absolute. And it is not by chance that Plato asserts, through the words of Phaedrus, that the one who loves is possessed by a god or by a religious frenzy. Desiring entails us not to completely belong to ourselves if we long for another living being.

More radically than knowledge, desire frees us, but it frees us by a link, and our freedom is effective only if the other gives us back to us as desiring; that is, if the other returns us to the absolute for which we are longing, and so absolves us from taking it as a possible object of our desire.

Our consciousness usurps the aim of our desire, it uses the quality of its energy and deprives us of the freedom that the absolute for which we long grants us. Our consciousness also grasps an energy that our desire is unable to use, because we lack a culture of the experience of desire. We have not yet let desire comes to its absolute, although it is probably that which most originally and after all allows us to be by uniting our body and our soul, our nature and culture, in an indissociable way. Desire corresponds to the real through which we can experience ourselves as being while letting it occur as it is. But the matter is no longer one of experiencing a word or a thought but a feeling—and what, then, occurs about perceiving as such. Moreover, what we have henceforth to perceive is not a thing but an other. And the other can be distinguished from the link that unites us with it less easily than a thing. In order that the other can appear as other, it is important that we distinguish our perception of it from that of ourselves. This can be achieved only by acknowledging and taking on a difference with regard to nature itself. If nature can provide us with a perception of the absolute it is thanks to a natural difference which allows us to perceive the other as the one who he or she is, that is, as absolutely other. No doubt, this perception cannot be immediately that of the other in its absolute, a frame must exist which makes such a perception possible. This operation needs an education—a dialectics?—of perception as a comprehensive phenomenon. We still lack it because we have separated intelligibility from sensitivity.

The Hegelian dialectics too quickly reduce our sensitive consciousness to an immediate process, whereas this consciousness is capable of mediation and self-affection. It can thus deal with an experience of itself and not merely remain at the service of the consciousness, as is imagined by Hegel. The point is that the self-experience regarding our sensitive perception occurs in the most absolute way through the mediation of an other. And if to know oneself knowing can correspond to a progress towards the knowledge of oneself as an absolute knowledge, it does not go the same regarding the experience of oneself as feeling. Experiencing the absolute then happens with difficulty without the other, including as an experience of immediacy.

It still remains for us to perceive and dialectize how immediacy can then correspond with the absolute, and how the becoming of the other can be linked with the becoming of oneself. Indeed, becoming oneself can give up neither experiencing oneself nor experiencing the other. It is the conjunction of these two experiences in immediacy which can grant us an experience of the absolute—which requires a certain progression and a resort to mediations on both sides. This also requires us to accept that the absolute cannot be experienced permanently, which does not mean it being relative. Nevertheless, each must take responsibility for the relative that it is absolutely in order to reach the experience of an absolute which is relative only with regard to an outside of the self but which is not relative in itself.

If in the Hegelian *Phenomenology* (Hegel 1966/1979) the spirit must appear to itself in order to accomplish itself, must become other to become itself, the same cannot apply to a phenomenology of desire. The question is no longer one of merely appearing to oneself, of appearing before oneself, but also of appearing to the other. And such appearing to the other does not amount to a real contradiction in comparison with appearing to oneself. Appearing to the other is necessary for a personal becoming which does not depend only on oneself, although it needs autonomy and self-affection. However, desire cannot be satisfied with a mere self-desire, but appearing to the other is not becoming the other either, even if it entails a risk of one's own disappearance in order that one should be recognized by the other.

Nevertheless, our appearing will not be overcome by another appearing, because the dialectical process is henceforth more complex. Appearing now calls for both a recognition by and a union with the other, which stops the motion of a projection onto a forward time or space and sends us back to ourselves, including to a natural belonging and a sensitive immediacy. Appearing amounts to our agreeing to be perceived in order to return to our own being and be born again.

The human being is originally split into two components. A dialectical process, which unfolds between us and an other naturally different from us, then substitutes, at least partly, for this resulting from a split between becoming oneself and becoming other. I am only an element of humanity, and letting myself be perceived by the other does not involve a contradiction between me as same as myself and me as different from myself, but it is a call for the recognition of a particularity which needs the desire of the other to fulfil a union at which I aim to accomplish my being.

In reality, the self-disclosure or turning out of our consciousness to itself only amounts to a partial accomplishment of ourselves. It does not yet correspond to the self-revelation and realization of our comprehensive being—desire better leads us to our complete fulfilment. And if, according to Hegel, reaching an absolute knowledge means the effectuation of both will and knowledge, it is nevertheless true that he subjects our will, or aspiration, to knowledge. Willing does not amount only to knowing, whatever the desire that we then experience. Wanting to be the ones who we are cannot be limited to knowing, including knowing our-selves—fulfilling our being longs for more. Moreover, even at the level of knowledge, such a fulfilment comes up against the impossibility of knowing the other as a knowing oneself. Experiencing the former is dif-ferent from experiencing the latter and requires the mediation of desire. And this experience, through which our being happens to itself, cannot occur without the other, and the knowledge, which can result from this, is of another nature from the Hegelian knowledge.

Now, what truly corresponds with the absolute for us is not only spirit but a more comprehensive being—the absolute for which we long is to fulfil our own to be. To reach this absolute cannot be gained through a mere experience of ourselves but calls for us to experience being with the other as a condition for our being to come or be dis-closed to itself. And this becoming with the other will also partly be a becoming the other, which demands our turning back to ourselves. But becoming other in the effective experience of our desire does not amount to the becoming other that consciousness, especially the Hegelian consciousness, experiences of itself when becoming other. The operation is more complex and asks of us to apply the negative to our being itself and not only to a stage of its appearing, an operation to which the dynamism of our will must make its contribution.

3

Elements of a Dialectics of Sensitivity

What Mood Allows Meeting the Other?

The other cannot be reduced to an object. Thus in order to be capable of meeting and taking into account the other, our consciousness must modify its traditional way of functioning. It no longer has to relate as a whole to an object; in other words, it no longer corresponds to the totality of the relation of an I, or a self, to an object, notably because it does not know such a totality. For this totality to come to appear as the one it is, the subject must have a relationship with a subject different from the one who he or she is by nature. In order that such a relationship should occur without losing one's self, this, from the very beginning, must be subjected to a negation—the frame which makes possible to meet the other as other is: I am not you. Subjecting our own being to a negation gives rise to the mood which enables us to deal with alterity. The absolute, then, is no longer merely intuited or projected, it is recognized as the reality to which it corresponds. Such a recognition allows me to aim at the absolute that I am without this absolute being for all that the absolute of the absolute. The other corresponds with an absolute too, on the condition that he or she takes on the non-being that

© The Author(s) 2019
L. Irigaray, *Sharing the Fire*,
https://doi.org/10.1007/978-3-030-28330-8_3

they are. Taking on such a negative, or a negation, allows a becoming other to oneself which is not mistaken for becoming the other. A structure exists which permits us both to relate to the other and to return to ourselves. Hence, I know the experience of the absolute from the very beginning, and relating to and with the other will allow me to cultivate this experience while preserving an absolute founded in nature.

'I am not you'—differently from 'I do not know you'—anticipates all the relativity which will happen in the relationship to and with the other, and prevents this relation from an indefinite drift or dissolution in the relative. Such a negative makes also possible that the difference remains qualitative, because the experience of the absolute then exempts our difference from being quantitative in order to resist a lack of differentiation. The absolute character of the negation preserves the living qualities of our being as an effective, and especially affective, part of our entire being.

This part is also the one which concerns the energy which underlies and keeps going the motion of becoming. And such an energy, or such a will, cannot be limited to a will to know. It involves a more comprehensive will—a will to live or a will to be. However, such a will cannot be fulfilled only from and by oneself, it needs to be accomplished with the other, which requires another logic. Beyond the fact that the negative, then, does not refer to a contrary or to an opposite, there is no longer a question of overcoming a presumed contradiction because the negative at stake is henceforth unsurmountable—to be will for ever be accompanied by a not-being. To be will also mean becoming oneself through a becoming the other, not only of the self but of the other.

Not being the other does not prevent us from experiencing something of the other, which alters us as a reality and a truth that we must recognize. Nevertheless, this reality or truth has become so intimate with our self that it is not certain that this self can ever be merely ours. Being oneself means agreeing to be also with the other, a being-with in which we must constantly assess what belongs to our being and to out non-being in order to safeguard our relation to the absolute regarding both life and transcendence.

Could this mean regarding life as transcendence? Not simply. No doubt we experience life as transcendence when we live it as an absolute. However, we have not yet defined or identified the frame which allows us to experience life as such towards its cultivation. Hence the referral to an absolute beyond life itself.

In order to cultivate the absolute that life represents, we must approach the nature of the finite and the infinite without losing ourselves in this distinction. All by myself I can experience the absolute, but this needs me to be limited in order to be kept alive while evolving. And it is an other who can provide me with both limit and limitlessness, an other who allows me to experience my life as finite but destined to develop thanks to relating to the infinite. The other who is capable of making me experience both my finiteness and infiniteness is above all an other who is differently sexuate. Indeed, this other reveals to me that my being is particular, thus finite, but it invites me to overcome such finiteness through the infinite to which desire summons me.

Such a call opens up the path towards the becoming of my being, a becoming which never will surmount the distress resulting from the irreducible dependence on finiteness. If such a distress compels me to live with wisdom, it also corresponds to what permits me to remain alive, that is, always in becoming—a becoming which must take into account sensitivity as a passage from empirical to transcendental. In other words, desire has not only to provide energy for the motion of becoming, it has also to provide a sensitive content capable of evolving.

In order to cultivate the relation of our sensitivity towards the absolute, self-affection seems to represent a way, or a method, of which self-consciousness would be only a stage. Self-affection provides us with a more comprehensive structure which allows us to dialectize a part of our being that self-consciousness is not able to take into account—as is the case in the Hegelian dialectics. Indeed, consciousness, as it is conceived by him, needs object(s) to experience itself, whereas self-affection can happen without any object and permits a further cultivation of subjectivity, notably at the sensitive level.

Cultivating intersubjective relations needs us to work out, and even to subject to a dialectical process, our sensitive experience. One could say that fulfilling our being cannot happen without us considering this part of ourselves, which moreover cannot be overcome by the objectivity of spirit. Life, its growth and its sharing require us to cultivate our sensitivity. Neglecting it or subjecting it to intelligibility do not allow us to achieve the potential of our being. Internalization and relationship to and with the other, in particular the other as a living being, necessitate the preservation and the transformation of our sensitivity not only as a medium and a mediation but also as a crucial aspect of our being. Our self cannot be limited to self-consciousness of a spiritual nature. It must remain sensitive and ensure the passage between our fleshly and our spiritual living being.

If the coming to itself of the spirit runs the risk of sinking down into monotony and uniformity it is because it neglects to take into account our sensitive part. The cultivation of our spirit must consider the aim and the development of this part of our being in order to take place without tediousness.

Desire must remain qualitatively sensitive if it intends to retain its connection to the absolute—in reality favouring quantity destroys this relation. Furthermore, if our desire strives to overcome the negation constitutive of our concrete being, it cannot achieve such a wish because the desire for the other cannot correspond to the absolute desire for oneself, or the desire for oneself as the absolute. What is more, desire must keep a relation to immediacy in order to have energy that it needs for its becoming—a mediation radically extraneous to an immediate experience would destroy the nature of desire. And removing the negation, or the negative, as far as desire is concerned, also amounts to destroying it.

Desire as desire for the absolute gets involved in a complex evolution between progression and going back. It must renounce any resort to the use of the desirable as a mediation aiming at abolishing alterity, without for all that giving up the desirable as a way to transform the natural energy. It must return to the source of its motion, and rediscover a path towards the absolute through experiencing a natural immediacy in order to work it out towards an absolute which takes into account the relationship with the other as other.

Henceforth, the mediation that is necessary is different from the one which is needed by a consciousness relating merely to itself. Desire asks us to renounce a mediation resorting only to object(s) and discover a mediation suitable for a relationship between subjects, with a sharing and not an appropriation or adequacy in mind. If desire was in search of an absolute knowledge, especially relative to our self, uniting with an other different from ourselves requires us to give up aiming at such an absolute. Longing for the absolute now necessitates the maintenance of the effectiveness of the negative and of a worry that nothing can soothe in an absolute way. Hence the endless motion of our becoming.

Energy as Sensitive Mediation

In reality our first desire does not long for knowledge but for a union with the other. We have then to deal with a double immediacy: one in the perception of the other, the second in the perception of the relation itself. The process of mediation is thus quite different from the Hegelian one. I cannot make the other appear only by myself, and I do not even have the measure and the terms which would allow me to discover its truth. The other cannot simply appear to me and, furthermore, it gives truth to itself.

I can make room for a horizon inside of which the other can appear without renouncing the immediacy of its sensitive life. As far as I am concerned, I must give up mediating all by myself the presence of the other through helping it to be. The mediation, then, results from assuming the negative of a difference which maintains the particularity of the life of each.

In reality, Hegel holds a dialogue with himself. He does not imagine that the knowledge to which he refers, the knowledge of and for himself, always involves also the truth of the other. He approaches truth only through his own way of mediating life. And yet the mediation in relating to and with the other requires us to represent the truth of the incarnation of our own life, including in its relational dimension. This entails our risking being in communication, even in communion, with the other and maintaining an immediacy in this communion, while mediating it in order that it should be in accordance with us as relating to this other. The immediacy of any communing with the other must turn into one favouring the conjunction between two different beings in order that it should end in a union in difference. Our energy can remain a natural energy which ensures the motion, although it is converted into one which makes possible a union with a different energy.

Energy must ensure both motion and mediation, which needs it to combine quality and quantity. In order that the dialectical process should go on, energy must also include a mobility and an intensity which are maintained by longing for the absolute. However, for being able to mediate the relation to the absolute, energy must be modulated by its quality—could I say by its tonality?—it must combine absolute and relative in a qualitative way.

In order that the absolute which corresponds only with one could be united with the absolute corresponding with the other(s), energy must be relativized with respect to one another by a quality other than this, or these, involved in the longing for the absolute itself. Such a quality must lead each from the perception of an absolute, which does not know itself as relative, to the perception of a relativity which discovers its relation as such to the absolute, notably through longing for the other as different. Indeed, in this way each opens up to an absolute more absolute, thus less relative, than the one for which each alone can long.

The necessity for a qualitative determination of our energy in order to mediate between two particular absolutes comes also from the fact that quality allows energy to preserve its immediacy and naturalness. Quality maintains the aptitude of energy for mediating without it being destroyed or transformed in an irreversible way; that is, it permits our energy to keep its sensitivity and its potential immediacy thanks to a transformation which safeguards it as such. This operation can happen only by cultivating energy as a medium which makes possible an experience of the absolute without being itself the absolute.

The dialectical process must thus be applied to the medium itself in order to maintain its ability to let our being be perceived without removing it from its living existence. This requires us to be capable of uniting the here and now of the one who perceives with those of the one who is perceived without cutting either of them off from their becoming absolutely the ones who they are. For the subject–object logic we thus need to substitute—or, at least we need to add on it—a logic regulated by the relationship between living beings, which can be worked out thanks to the mediation and the medium provided by a natural energy humanly cultivated so that it should be shareable. Following Hegel, but differently from him, I could say that the 'I' who perceives 'this' must receive from such a 'this' its this-me as living, which can occur in a meeting with any living being, but can be accomplished in an absolute way only when meeting a human being who is differently sexuate. Indeed, only he or she can give me back to my me as a differentiated this-me able to perceive in an absolute way another living being as the one who it is—a process in which the relative here and now of each is referred to the absolute to which it longs in a specific way.

The work of Hegel lacks a true dialectics of the sensitive knowledge in particular because he conceives it starting from one subject only. Thus he does not take into account the mediation which already exists in the sensitive experience. And this happens at three levels: (1) he does not imagine that the fact of being a 'this' capable of sensitive perception presupposes a mediation of life itself; (2) he does not really envision receptiveness and passivity as a means of knowledge; (3) he does not take into account the medium which permits knowledge at a sensitive level.

Probably all these aporias result from the fact that Hegel does not consider enough the experience of sensitivity between two living subjects. He particularly neglects the motion and the mediation already at stake in such an experience. He envisages the sensitive certainty only through apprehending an object already deprived of life by a consciousness which, also, is cut off from life. The 'this' of what is perceived, as well as the one who perceives, in fact, are produced by a logic which does not truly care about life itself. And what Hegel calls sensitivity amounts to a sort of physical reaction in a kind of laboratory for experimentation. Immediacy itself is then artificial and, as such, motionless, insensitive or aseptic, thus unable to ensure any mediation.

Through his recapitulation of the history of Western philosophy, Hegel shows how much its manner of thinking has neglected to consider life itself as mediating and mediated in a particular way in/by different living beings. Hence, he needs three absolutes to objectively support the achievement of consciousness: art, religion and philosophy. But Hegel deprives in this way the living beings that we are of a dynamic and shareable connection to the absolute necessary for our becoming. Indeed, immediacy is envisioned by Hegel in the relation(s) between subject and object(s), in which it no longer exists as really alive. It is already subjected to a cultural mediation which determines our consciousness and makes it exist only through a relation to an object and vice versa.

In such a configuration, immediacy already results from a construction and is not truly immediate. Thus the matter no longer consists in the fact that any present experience is only an example of the particularity of a 'this' in comparison with that which would be the essence of immediacy.

In reality, experiencing immediacy is now dependent on another logic in which the copula is of use to unite two subjects naturally different instead of uniting a subject with object(s). By favouring the relation to object(s), the subject loses the possibility of experiencing an immediacy founded in nature. This can take place only thanks to the cultivation of an experience of immediacy between two living beings; that is, thanks to the working out of the sensitive experience that a subject lives in meeting with another living subject.

A real immediacy is experienced in an energy communion with another living being in which the immediacy which is experienced by each has already been transformed in order to become shareable. Immediacy can be experienced only as already mediated not through a differentiation between a subject and object(s) but through the natural difference existing between two subjects. As such, it cannot be interpreted as an example of the experience of real life in comparison with an essence but as the return to the universality of life which, as an absolute, can be experienced by becoming incarnate through the difference between living beings.

Hegel produces difference or differentiation instead of acknowledging and mediating a natural difference which already exists. In this way he deprives us of an experience of immediacy as a possible mediation towards our becoming the ones who we are. Hegel, as other philosophers before and after him, creates a differentiation internal to the subject in order not to be confronted with the unsurmountable difference and negative that the natural difference between our sexuate belongings represents. However, this difference could return him to himself as a determined subject who wanted to be, who had to form a world, and even to gain a consciousness, through relating to a subject naturally different from himself.

About Universality of Sensitive Experience

Hegel approaches sensitive knowledge starting from the subject–object relation. Now this way of conceiving the frame for tackling the subject–subject relation looks inappropriate, notably regarding the question of the 'here' and 'now'. The object that Hegel gives as an example is always presumed to be an inanimate object from which the spatiotemporal dimension is assessed. However, in the subject–subject relation, the 'now' is not the same for each apart from in an abstract and not universal way. For example, the 31 January at 6.00 p.m. is not experienced in the same way by the one who was born 5, 15, 30 or 50 years ago—and any universal can overcome this difference. The same goes for the 'here'. The examples set by Hegel determine the 'here' starting from a place opposite the subject. And yet we do not each have the same before ourselves when we are opposite each other. And, unless we do not take into account the experience itself, we have each the other opposite ourselves. Hence the impossibility of sharing the same 'here'.

Thus the point is not to define the sensitive certainty starting from a universal presumed to be common, but to recognize that it must always be extraneous to, and one could say ecstatic with respect to, an eventual presumed universal. And this does not have the same effect at the level of knowledge. My knowledge then remains relative whatever the absolute nature of what I experience. In reality, no object can correspond with the sensitive certainty except this that I made not only through the absolute nature of my knowledge but as its being itself. In this case, is it really a question of a sensitive experience and knowledge?

By subjecting any 'this' to universality, especially that of language, Hegel removes it from an immediate sensitive experience. The only common 'this' that is truly sensitive is perhaps the one which occurs, or ought to occur, in the embrace between two subjects. Such a 'this' corresponds to a potentially universal experience for human beings but not as one being made universal by language—except sometimes by an artistic one?

If embracing is at the real root of our saying, no language, at least already existing, can tell it. Potentially universal, the 'this' present in our hugging one another cannot be made universal, and no language, no discourse can pretend to substitute for its particular embodiment. The memory of an experience of carnal embrace is entrusted to the body, and no other language can ensure its durability as such. One could say that such a 'this' cannot become a 'that' on pain of losing its meaning. It cannot take place or fade away merely as an active production or as passive effects—as works or affects, notably pathological ones—either. This experience must remain as a remembrance which contributes to the occurrence of a future 'this' through its transformation into a past 'this'. Such a working out is complex on several accounts, and we lack mediations to carry it out. We cannot even aim simply at a future 'this' because nothing can really guarantee its happening as such.

Desire henceforth is no longer the desire of a subject in relation to an object, but the dynamic opening up to a risky encounter between two longings. If one part of such a meeting, the sexuate attraction, seems to be capable of being universal at the carnal, but not the linguistic, level, the shaping up and the incarnation of the longing can be foreseen with difficulty in their 'here' and 'now'. The two longings must learn how to be dialectized by one another without reducing themselves to one another—something that sexuate difference can grant us thanks to its way of determining our subjectivity.

It is above all sexuation which permits us to dialectize our incarnation. Hence, the dialectical process no longer amounts to holding a dialogue with oneself—as is the case in Hegel's and even already in Plato's method whatever appearances—it unfolds through a dialogue with the other. The sensitive experience is then of a quite other nature. First, because aiming at an object and longing for another subject do not obey the same logic. Whatever the longing for the absolute that they inspire in me, I cannot make the other truly mine. Nevertheless, in my desire for him, or for her, they are my wanting and energy which are involved. In my relation to and with the other a 'mine' is thus committed. In order not to completely lose this 'mine' in the desire that

I experience for the other, I must—differently from what is needed by the method advocated by Hegel—renounce making the other mine. In other words, I cannot absolve myself from my desire for the other, because it keeps living my longing for the absolute, including in its immediacy. Such a motion is almost the opposite of that at work in the Hegelian dialectics. Longing for the absolute now requires us to definitively give up making our own, subjectively or objectively, the one who is desired, above all at the level of consciousness.

No doubt something occurs in me thanks to the desire for, and also of, the other. But that which occurs cannot be appropriated by my consciousness on pain of relativizing my desire, of depriving it of its relation to the absolute and its dynamic potential. In order that desire should keep such properties, it cannot be reduced to a conscious process, although it has to be memorized for its becoming. Such memorization must preserve a potential immediacy without thwarting its durability—which is allowed by a physical inscription. This requires a certain passivity, but one to which we actively agree and that we assume.

In order that my desire should persevere in its search for the absolute, I must accept being touched by the other and affected by this other in a lasting way, but with an evolution of myself in mind. Experiencing then does not divide up between feeling and acting, it is a moment of the dialectical motion towards fulfilling desire. And the stronger is my capability for feeling, the stronger also is my longing for the absolute. Obviously feeling in this case cannot mean a mere suffering, as it has too often been conceived in our tradition, but rather a necessary stage towards the fulfilment of our desire. Indeed the latter cannot content itself with activity or passivity—especially when they are distributed between the masculine and the feminine—but it needs a link between the active and the passive in each one, in order that a motion should go from being affected to being willing from each and in each. This ensures the permanence of desire in the motion of each towards the absolute, and a possible sharing, more exactly a possible communion, in such a process.

This too rarely happens for lack of a cultivation of our comprehensive being and a method capable of ensuring such a cultivation. At least two reasons, amongst others, can be put forward to explain this lack: the subjection of sensitivity to intelligibility, and the passage from one to many without consideration for what occurs in the relationship between two. These two characteristics of our tradition bear witness to the importance attached to a making outside of ourselves to the detriment of a becoming of ourselves, and our consequent laceration between diverse realizations.

For example, when Hegel alludes to interiority, it is already to a mental process that he refers, a process which does not take into account a longing for the absolute of our global being, but considers only that of our consciousness. Hence, the fact that the Hegelian dialectics can unfold in spite of a subjection of sensitivity to mind and the passage from one to many without the stage of the relation between two, whatever its crucial importance for our comprehensive accomplishment. Indeed, the cultivation of this relation is what allows us to deal with and to transform immediacy into a means which preserves its immediate nature without bending it to a construction which mediates it in a more or less artificial way.

Here and Now in Intersubjective Relations

Desire, more generally any relation between two naturally different humans, requires, in order to be shared, a deconstruction of the Hegelian dialectical process. It requires us to return to a specific personal experience, to an artlessness liberated from any universalizing elaboration. It needs us to recover the immediacy of a natural perception which still acknowledges difference(s). Such deconstruction, or negative ontology, runs the risk of falling back into a lack of differentiation too, which, then, is due to an attraction which abolishes the duality of subjectivities and identities through a fusion, a domination or a subjection, and even through a communion which amounts to a blind immersion in an undifferentiated whole.

That which has been deconstructed must be re-elaborated starting from the difference of nature existing between the subjects. Any universal construction may neglect this problem and leap over the stage of its possible solution. But the universality does not correspond to the same on every side, and desire, more generally relationship, cannot be put into the neuter without being harmed and even destroyed. The operation which will permit our sharing is a transformation, by each, of an immediacy into another that is more original, more virgin but, nevertheless, not put into the neuter. The important thing is to keep energy alive and shareable as such.

If the motion in the Hegelian dialectics needed the splitting of our subjectivity and the neutralizing, at least partly, of our energy in order that it should unfold, the dialectics suitable for cultivating the relation between two naturally different subjects, needs each of them to beware of being split and to keep their energy unified, the two subjectivities as well as their energies being determined in a different way. Henceforth, it is another process which is at stake, and it is no longer resorting to reflection which can contribute towards its developing. Sexuate difference cannot be subjected to reflection, and when we subject it to reflection it loses its effectiveness because it aims at uniting with the other but not at becoming other in and for each in order to be assumed as a oneself.

The scission which is entailed by sexuation is not one between me and myself, at least it is the case when sexuate difference preserves the absolute that my desire wants to reach. There is then the question of a scission between the other and me, and if unhappiness exists, it results from the separation from one another. This separation is unsurmountable, but it is such a negative, this not being the other, which permits the union between us to keep our desire aspiring after the absolute, and to happen as a non-controllable and imperfect overcoming of the scission with which our being has to deal in an absolute way.

Belonging to only one genus causes both our unhappiness and our happiness in a process in which a definitive reconciliation will never happen. Thus our anxiety will never be completely soothed except by denying our irreducible difference. This can take various forms: confining ourselves to sameness, to equality, to one only identity, but also attributing the negative to the other or charging this other of the negative in an active or passive way, acting and thinking in a supposedly sexless manner, promoting a universal culture lacking in sexuate differentiation, favouring reproduction to the detriment of desire, keeping desire in abeyance by supra-sensitive ideals and so on.

The Hegelian dialectics aims at reducing difference to sameness. However, the difference that Hegel endeavours to overcome is a difference with which he already provided himself and not the difference which really exists between subjects differently determined by nature. And yet if longing for the absolute remains a constituent of our subjectivity, it is because the longing which supports the motion of the dialectical process is itself underpinned by a desire to be more fundamental than the desire to know. This desire to be brings energy to our will to know more about being, and the former is in a way sacrificed to the latter. Nevertheless, the absolute after which this latter aspires cannot be absolved from the absolute after which our desire to be aspires, a desire which continues wanting to develop, and which stops its motion only by splitting itself into aiming at art, religion and philosophy. Maintaining such difference results only from an operation of our subjectivity which does not allow this subjectivity to escape its own fragmentation.

The unity of subjectivity in its search for the absolute can be safeguarded by bowing before a difference that it cannot overcome; that is, by bowing to an unsurmountable negative. And this corresponds to the properly human undertaking that we have to achieve—a task from which humanity never stops shrinking, notably by concealing the negative in diverse forms of absolutes of which we cannot have an experience, such as supra-sensitive ideals and God himself. We have also hidden the negative in a so-called common sense, lacking in differentiation, to which we ought to submit and which is presumed to embody the universality of our condition. But it only represents a partial embodiment of this condition at a given epoch of history.

This is particularly obvious and problematic when it is a question of truth with regard to the other. In order to exempt ourselves from taking on the negative of an insurmountable difference, we perceive this other through supra-sensitive ideals or the neutralization of a presumed common sense; that is, we do not perceive him or her as they are. Their current presence remains hidden from us by various cultural constructions, so that it escapes from our perception and we are led to fragment it for glimpsing something of it. We no longer perceive the being of the other but only some modalities of its embodiment: citizen, worker, family member, sexual partner and so on. We are then allowed to include this other as spare parts within the horizon of our own world without assuming the negative which permits us to meet this other as a comprehensive being. The place thanks to which we could return to one another our own being and seek how to join our two different beings is then taken away from us.

Certainly, the negative cannot be assumed either once and for all or always in the same way. For example, in order to perceive the other as other, that is, as different, I must immerse myself in myself—Hegel perhaps would say that I must sink into myself—but also in the perception of the other and, next, be able to restore the limits of each of us. And it is not a dialectics in which only our consciousness is involved which could carry out such a process. A cultivation of passivity and of its combination with activity, notably at the physical and sensitive levels, is needed in order to recognize the other as other.

The mere acceptance of the difference of the other presupposes that we assume an irreducible passivity accompanied by an insurmountable negative. However, such a passivity, as well as this negative, have a positive function in the constitution of our subjectivity. They provide it with a unity which contributes to gathering other properties which are incapable, only by themselves, of making up such a unity, given their relative lack of significance for one another and in relation to other entities. Thus they could compose a unity only through a co-belonging which lacks necessity and stability or permanence. The potential for uniting needs a more irreducible property, including at the natural level, a property which is not indifferent either to its own unity or to the unities with which it has to deal outside of itself. Sexuate difference corresponds to such a property.

Acknowledging the intervention of sexuate difference in the unification of our subjectivity entails agreeing that the latter is determined in a way that is both particular and not indifferent to the whole that we constitute, as well as not indifferent to the world in which we are, and in particular to the other sexuate being with whom we compose humanity. Besides, this unification of subjectivity through its non-indifference allows the dialectical process to preserve a qualitative element without submitting either to neutralization or to mere quantitative phases towards a passage to the absolute.

The Qualitative Truth of Our Being

Henceforth, opposition is no longer that which can safeguard the qualitative dimension in our aiming at the absolute through overcoming contradictions. The negative no longer operates as a way of determining by excluding. It corresponds to the recognition of the existence of a difference which maintains each one within its limits. Thus it is no longer a question of progressing towards truth or right by dismissing falsehood or wrong, but of not pretending that we are what or who we are not, firstly by nature. Indeed, what is specific to us is originally granted us by nature, and how to perceive and cultivate it must inspire the motion of our becoming.

This requires us to put the stress on the manner of entering into relation with the fruitful respect for our difference(s) in mind, instead of focusing on excluding what is inappropriate. What or who we are exists from the outset. Becoming requires us to embody the ones who we are, but not the one who the other is, while developing the relational properties which are ours through growing by being in relation with the other(s). It is between subjects that the negative must be applied in order to maintain their respective reality, truth and progression towards their accomplishment as different from one another. Desire provides us with a motion the stake of which is not to exclude a presumed opposite in order to become ourselves, but to preserve the/our difference in order that the motion of becoming lives on. No doubt this task is not easy, but it is probably the most distinguishing feature of humanity.

What such an undertaking requires us to carry out is more complex than what is needed by the Hegelian dialectical process. Indeed, if I long for the other it is because I long for him or her as necessary for my own fulfilment. However, the other is not an object and my consciousness cannot act towards him or her as towards an object—the difference between the other and myself is more radically objective though it can be less objectively defined at the subjective level. The other is naturally different from me and I cannot become this other, but my desire for the other makes it subjectively intimate with me. I must preserve the desire for the other as a desire for a beyond that I cannot become, even if it partakes in my being. Instead of excluding the other from myself as an unsuitable object, my desire must aim at rendering mine what of him or her allows me, and even both, to develop towards a more and more absolute union; that is, at rendering mine what favours my perception of and my desire for the other as other. In other words, one could say that I must endeavour to perceive the other not as an object but as a subject, and a subject different from myself—as a necessary partner of my accomplishment. Thus the dialectical process no longer applies to the relation between a subject and an object but to the relation between two subjects objectively different.

As there is then no object at which one aims, that one wants to take and appropriate, or even to which one wants to appropriate oneself, the motion is more complex and may exhaust itself or be dashed in its search for the absolute. Thus it would be useful to sustain its development by qualitative supports, which both temper and keep the motion going without letting the absolute alone be the guarantor of the quality of becoming. Some pauses are necessary too, some moments of embodiment, and also some sensitive perceptions which make possible our aiming at the absolute while taking on the negative, without, nevertheless, being destroyed.

The negative must procure to the living beings that we are a space–time in which to dwell, to open out, to experience ourselves as a flesh and to fulfil the ones who we are. The function of such a negative is not to perpetuate a logic of opposites, of contraries, of exclusion and so on; rather it must ensure a unity in which qualitative properties can be experienced, combine with one another, evolve in order to be able to unite with a different unity, that of the other. The qualitative effect of what is perceived of the other then intervenes as an assessment which substitutes for judgement(s), the criteria of which are more or less overtly quantitative.

Our sexuation allows us to gather various properties of the living being that we are which, for lack of such gathering, would either fragment almost indefinitely or be united by criteria extraneous to

life itself, which, as such, would destroy our physical and carnal qualities notably by quantitative evaluations. These could express themselves
through domination, competition and so on which would supplant the
sensitive experience of quality. In Hegelian terms, it could be possible to
say that sexuation permits us to correspond with a universal mediation
while keeping this alive and able to evolve. This can occur only by preserving its specificity—in this case, its sexuate character.

Sexuate belonging has a really particular property because the for
oneself that it can supply is also a for the other, before any reference to
an other or a multiple external to oneself. As such, sexuation can ensure
the unity of the subject while opening up this subject to the other, so
that each, by becoming oneself, should also become for the other. This
aptitude of sexuation is in a way unique: unifying me it also provides
me with a mediation to relate to and with the other. Moreover, mediating in this way between us as different, my sexuate belonging puts also
the other itself in relation to/with me. The 'for you' becomes a potential
'for me'.

Henceforth, the perception of otherness is no longer based on quantity but on quality: an external quality relative to the being of the other,
but also an internal quality corresponding to what my flesh perceives
of this other. It is not whatever other that I can perceive as 'my' other,
but an other who, whilst it remains transcendentally different from me
through its sexuation, can also potentially be united with me—one
could say, conjoined to me—because it is possible that it would be
joined to my being without destroying what this being is truly and can
become. Quantity, including quantity of the affect, must remain sec-
ondary in comparison with quality. It is the latter which determines the
other as being potentially 'my' other, whereas the other who appeals to
me through quantity falls back into the status of one amongst others, so
losing the particularity of its otherness for me—as well as for itself. It,
then, too, loses its inherent status of universal mediation.

The potential of sexuation as universal mediation is also unique with
regard to the negative. If sexuation contributes to the unity both of the
one and of the other, it can act in this way only if each assumes the
fact of not being the other—the for oneself for the other that it grants
requires the assumption of such a negative. As such it is probably the

most specifically human mediation and the only one able to substitute for supra-sensitive ideals in the process of our becoming. Indeed, the mediation corresponding to sexuation needs, in order to be effective, the acknowledgement of an unsurmountable negative, the nature of which is qualitative, whereas the nature of the passage to an absolute depending on supra-sensitive ideas or ideals is basically quantitative, and it can eventually be overcome in another existence. In other words, sexuation asks of us to agree to long for an absolute which is for ever objectively relative.

This sends us back to our condition of living being, for which the absolute remains always particular and must be recognized as such in order to be effective. However, such an absolute is only externally relative, and this relativity allows each of us to come closer to the absolute which corresponds to ourselves through an internal development. It is because I am not the other that I can perceive this other not only as an object of my consciousness but as another living human subjectivity for which I may long. And what I experience at the sensitive level, notably by being in communion with the other, amounts to a stage of my becoming that I must transform as such through a dialectical process.

How can we succeed in that? How can we keep living the negative which maintains the individualization of the one and of the other and gives each of us back to a self-affection which does not preclude hetero-affection? Of what, including dialectical, cultivation of sensitivity— and proprioceptivity?—are we in need to carry out such a process? For lack of it, does not our experience of desire and love run the risk of being reduced to a mere pathology?

For Me for You; for You for Me

Logic is, then, no longer based on an equation such as 'a' is equal to 'b', at which 'a' aims as its objective corresponding, but on 'a' is 'a' and is different from 'b'. 'A' as equal to 'a' is given by nature, but it must come true, and it needs 'b', as a different being with which it must be conjoined, in order to be. Thus 'a' aims at 'b' as a mediation towards the absolute after which it aspires. However, contrary to what occurs in a Hegelian dialectics, 'b' is the mere support of a mediation towards the absolute for which 'a' longs. Only the embodiment of the mediation itself could correspond to the absolute after which 'a' aims, but it is never achieved in an absolute way, at least definitively.

Unlike a logic based on 'a' must become equal to 'b', the latter being what objectively determines 'a', logic is henceforth based on 'a' is equal to 'a', 'b' is equal to 'b' but different from 'a', and 'a' conjoined with 'b' is the place where the absolute can take place. It is after the union of 'a' with 'b', as different from 'a', that the desire for the absolute aspires. And yet, the union of 'a' with 'b' is never absolutely accomplished, even if the absolute can be experienced through it. Hence, we can continue to long for the absolute, because it never becomes definitely embodied, which supports our becoming. This can also correspond to the contribution to a community and to the history of those who work on such embodiment because they so contribute towards the evolution of the question concerning being.

Logic henceforth is based on assuming difference in order to produce or reproduce human being. This needs to resort to a triple dialectical process. Indeed, if 'a' is equal to 'a', it must also become the one that it is thanks to a dialectical process between a natural given and a cultural development—and it is the same for 'b'. The fact of not being faithful to becoming the ones that they are leads them to a sort of pathological contradiction which paralyses the motion of their development. Nevertheless, becoming the ones who they are asks them to compromise with the different from themselves. This could also be expressed in the following way: I cannot become absolutely myself without being also with the other. The participation of the other is needed by the motion towards my own becoming.

This puts a further question concerning my longing for the absolute. Such a question cannot be limited to a mere speculative interrogation and cannot be solved—Hegel perhaps would say that it cannot be absolved—at a solely spiritual level. Desire takes root in the body and cannot be completely distinguished from it. No doubt, energy can be transformed, it can become more subtle and more compatible with the nature of the transcendental. However, it cannot become completely incorporeal on pain of abolishing the evolution of life itself and the respect for alterity—something that our tradition mistakenly did. Hence a necessary return to its foundation, its definition of being and its method.

According to our past logic, a subject could decide on its determinations. And yet if we take seriously into account our sexuation, notably starting from our experience but also from scientific experimentations, we must admit that sexuation determines our subjectivity before any determination that we can freely allot to ourselves. Although this is often denied, all of our subjective choices and late determinations will be sexuated. Subjectivity cannot attribute its determinations only by itself, it is also assigned by them. Acknowledging that we are determined by our sexuate belonging grants us a margin of freedom with regard to logical functioning.

This also allows us to recover a dynamism arising from our nature itself instead of it being allocated by understanding. From then on, the logical link as syntax itself will be first concerned with the connection between subjects, and subjects which are different, but not with the connection between a subjectivity and its object(s) or other determination(s). And this frees the copula from its subjection to an objective external estimation and gives back to it an ontological status with regard to the subjects and their relationships.

To be, then, is defined by our origin and our relational belonging, notably in comparison with other subjects, more than by a relation to object(s) on which understanding decides. The absolute is no longer to be sought through reaching adequacy between objectivity and subjectivity, between an external objective aim of the subject and the accomplishment of subjectivity. Rather, the absolute is experienced in an ecstatic relationship between us, as naturally determined subjects, an ecstasy in which our origin endeavours to achieve its finality again. In a way such achievement is unattainable, but we dynamically long for it and this requires a dialectical process which does not implicate only consciousness and speculation but also the body, sensitivity and flesh as such, in accordance with their different incarnations in the one and in the other.

How is it possible to introduce such dialectics? Hegel subjects the sensitive to the supra-sensitive without a dialectical treatment of sensitivity itself. Yet, if understanding begins with phenomena, it subjects them to reasoning, removing them in this way from their sensitive properties. Besides, Hegel thinks little about the fact that the appearing of a living being is not first for an other but corresponds to a stage of its becoming—a flower does not flower for me, but because flowering corresponds to its being a flower.

The matter is that Hegel considers such a flowering to be above all for him, what is more as an object of knowledge. He could live this appearing of the flower at a sensitive level, experience it with his comprehensive being and so transform his mode of knowing, but he does not act in this way. He neither questions nor cultivates the passive receptiveness which takes place when one contemplates a flower and the subjective internalization which can result from such apperception. He leaps over it towards a supra-sensitive level.

And the matter is still more complex when it is a question of a sensitive meeting between two human beings, especially if they are differently sexuated. Indeed, if its appearing is, for each of them, a for-itself—and even an in-itself-for-itself—it can also be a for-the-other. However, this phenomenon must remain sensitive in order for it not to be cut off either from the self or from the other. It must be taken as a sensitive sign towards a conjunction with one another. It cannot be extrapolated from its sensitive nature in order to maintain its own development, and that of both. It is in the relation itself that the motion of becoming must find its impetus, but not through reasoning, rather through a sensitive perception and its evolving by meeting at a sensitive level, especially between two differently sexuated humans. Then experiencing, more than knowing, acts as mediation.

Moreover, one could object to Hegel that conceiving of the absolute as knowledge involves a contradiction, because knowledge seems to solve the question of the absolute, whereas the absolute and knowledge are not situated at the same level. The absolute is that for which subjectivity longs, which underlies the motion and ensures, in various guises, a mediation in the dialectical process. Nevertheless, Hegel intends to stop the motion of this process by assuming that the absolute for which we long is knowledge. However, knowledge does not completely fulfil our desire for the absolute and, for lack of being treated in a dialectical way, this desire risks falling back into the absolute of a sensitive immediacy. Knowledge as such cannot absolve us from our longing for the absolute, because we long for another absolute.

We cannot reach alone, through a mere mediation of spirit, the absolute for which we long. In our worrying search, we often entrust our thirst for the absolute to the other or to the Other, unless we defer it to some supra-sensitive ideal. Searching for the absolute in the other or in the Other, we are not only in search of an absolute knowledge. Rather, we are in search of an absolute of being that we hope we will reach through a communion or a union, which amongst other things approaches the mystery of our origin.

However, the communion or union for which we are longing in an absolute way, after which our subjectivity aspires and towards which it strives as much as is possible, is confronted with the objective partiality of our participation in being—not in a Being more or less differentiated and determined, but in the human being that we differently incarnate, especially according to our sexuate belonging. Hence the necessity for a return to an original pathos instead of suspending it in the various pathological repercussions of the repression of our attractions and desires.

4

The Absolute After Which Desire Aspires

Towards a Non-pathological Pathos

We can discover or rediscover a genuine pathos through a cultivation of our sensory perceptions. This requires us to procure a unity for them and for ourselves from the impact that they have on us. Certain practitioners of yoga—such as Patanjali or Roger Clerc, to name only two of them—took an active interest in a possible unification of our various sensory perceptions, as is also the case with some western artists—for example, Paul Klee. It is then a matter of discovering in us a place able to gather and metabolize the diverse effects on us of these perceptions in order that they do not transform us into a field of forces fighting over the privilege of determining us.

We have in ourselves another element of our sensitivity capable of unifying us in an authentic way and from the inside: our sexuate belonging. The latter has a potential that we have too little taken into account, although it represents a crucial aspect of our pathos, and a pathos at once unifying. As Freud states, sexuate belonging does not only concern sexuality strictly speaking but our global being. Nevertheless, and like most of those who approached the question of

© The Author(s) 2019
L. Irigaray, *Sharing the Fire*,
https://doi.org/10.1007/978-3-030-28330-8_4

sensitivity, Freud treats sexuation as a pathology more than as the possible foundation of a new cultivation of human being, both more elaborate and more achieved.

It is true that this asks for a real cultural evolution, the logic and language of which are still to be discovered and carried out. For example, when some of the last philosophers—like Maurice Merleau-Ponty or Michel Henry—approach the domain of sensuous relationships, they basically confine themselves to a subject-object logical structure, without considering what occurs between two subjects. And when such a relationship is envisioned it is more often than not according to a master-slave, dominant-dominated scheme which aims at nullifying at least one of the two subjectivities. None really thinks about the sensitive perceptions that the desire of/for the other arouses in us, perceptions in which it is sometimes difficult to distinguish between what is experienced by one and what is experienced by the other. Hegel does not wonder about this subtle differentiation between the for-oneself and the for-the-other in our attractions and their expression—which ought to have compelled him to make the dialectical process more complex. Hegel does not imagine that the internal unity with which sexuation can provide us represents a for-oneself but also a for-the-other, no side of which can be overcome by/in the other. Indeed, there is no contradiction in this duality of the for-oneself and the for-the-other, and it must be maintained in order that desire should exist and its strength make effective our sexuate identity.

For all that, must a more or less conflicting, and even contradictory, set of forces to exist, which both our way of conceiving of our sexuate identities as opposite and the motion of the Hegelian dialectics would need? Not at all. Rather, it is a matter of defining another dialectics because, in the motion of the Hegelian dialectics, unity is reached through a process which is mainly dependent on the assessment of consciousness and understanding, which subjects the real to already constructed categories—for example, subject and object—in order to institute a totality.

In our past logic, every connection is dependent on such rules. Certainly Hegel, unlike Kant, is in search of what would be the final universal unity, but he remains within a logic which, in a way, prevents him from discovering it. Indeed, he looks out for this last gathering through the connection between subject and object(s) instead of between subjects. What is more, object(s) then at stake is/are predetermined by consciousness and not given by nature. Thus Hegel supplies himself with an a priori final unity that he will endeavour to reach, and so he puts our being in the service of his way of thinking.

And yet, nature provides us with an original and final unity, the one from which we were born and which we try to incarnate with the other who is different from us by nature. Even if we would confine ourselves to the subject–object logic, the object would thus be given to us by nature, and determining this object according to our consciousness or our knowledge would amount to using the negative as we please—and this could only produce nothingness. Moreover, the subject-object logical structure would still rule over our sensitive, especially our sexual, relations between subjects differently sexuated. Nature would then be subjected to our traditional culture without being cultivated as such—which distorts the truth of the one and of the other.

This also prevents judgement from arbitrating with justice and equity on the possible mediation between the one and the other, be they man and woman, or more generally culture and nature. Consequently, to be and not to be are unequally and unfairly distributed between them, which not only perverts the relation between them but also that which can unite them.

So, and without going further than desire, there is no doubt that this aspires after an additional being arising from a not yet being. Desire needs both a 'to be' and a 'not to be' in order to exist, and the other will be the support of this aspiration. A dialectical process can make appear whether this 'not-to be' is a not yet being or an absolute not being. This asks for an assessment which cannot amount to what Hegel defines as an operation of understanding for several reasons: reflection then is no longer of great help; the other never will be mine, including at the level of intellect; there is no contradiction between two differently sexuated humans and so on. It is on the possible mediation of desire and its potential for achieving or not a union between us that the question must focus; thus, in a way, on the motion itself as being capable or not of leading us to unite with one another towards the accomplishment of our 'to be'.

Undoubtedly, reaching unity is now what is sought, as much for each as between the two, which certainly raises a problem but does not really amount to a contradiction. It is henceforth a matter of evolving through a transformation postulated from our origin: desire between us is firstly a natural datum. However, our aspiration after the absolute must remain undetermined and is dependent on each assuming two negatives: (1) one is not and never will be the other; (2) the unity that one can compose with the other is dependent on each taking on the fact, both real and true, that neither of them corresponds to the whole of the human being. If the absolute, that I sometimes experience in the union with the other, is more absolute than the one which I can live only by myself, it can be experienced only by agreeing to give up being the whole of being, that is, by assuming an irreducible non-being.

I cannot become the other, and taking on this negative supports my desire. The body of the other is irreducible to mine, at least as a living being. It is at such a price that my desire exists, remains sensitive and can ensure an effective mediation between the other and myself. The transcendence of the other for which I long, especially as a desire to be, entails that my longing reaches a transcendental level while remaining sensitive.

From Subordination to Conjunction

The fact that the absolute henceforth corresponds with the absolute of our 'to be' means that desire acts as a mediation not only between elements of our own being but between two natural and spiritual being(s) without us having to resort to any object—one could say to any having. As well as making our way towards the absolute as the nature of transcendence to accomplish our being as human is now quite another thing. It is no longer a matter of mastering anything, especially by consciousness, but of acknowledging and letting be the transcendence existing in nature itself as a result of the irreducible difference between our being(s) and of its cultivation towards the ec-stasis of our union. This calls for a transformation of the content and the form of our desire so that the desire of one could be in harmony with the desire of the other. In search of a possible and provisory union, one cannot dominate or subject the other to oneself. For example, one cannot intend to be merely an 'I' addressing a 'you'; each must in turn, and even simultaneously, be both 'I' and 'you'—which thwarts the reduction of anyone to an object and preserves the duality of subjectivities. This also protects the peculiarity of the desire of each, a desire which is never empty or abstractly universal but which aims at a union with respect for difference(s). In this union the most elusive of our origin is joined to the most elusive of our search for the absolute.

Such an absolute cannot be reached through using the copula—to be—at the most radical, and even intensive, stage of adequacy in the relation between a subject and an object. It is the relationship between two subjects which now aims at the absolute. And this presupposes another meaning of the word 'to be' and of its copulating use. If its function was in a way to assess the correctness of a link of subordination in the relation between a subject and an object, it is now to carry out a conjunction between two subjects—to be expressing the achievement of such a conjunction. This 'to be', at which we then aim, is both sensitive and transcendental, and it allows each to preserve its being from remaining in a sensitive immediacy and from being subjected to supra-sensitive ideals or processes in order to reach the absolute—a motion which henceforth borrows its dynamism from a natural energy which is cultivated towards uniting with one another.

Another important aspect in such a dialectics regarding sensitiveness is that it takes place, at least originally, between two beings differently determined by nature. Thus the question is no longer one of unifying a multiplicity of properties with their integration into a unity in mind, but of allowing different natural determinations to combine with one another towards a more accomplished unity without one ever becoming the other, because this would deprive them of a relation to the absolute of their union.

The necessity of such a union has little to do with mere understanding, even if our culture has tried to bend it to this requirement, notably by subjecting uniting with one another to procreation. And yet, our union as such is extraneous to procreation, and reducing it to the latter amounts to subjecting it to a natural law which is not yet raised to a human state. No doubt, uniting with one another can generate, but it ought first to generate us regardless of any procreation. And this additional deed with respect to our union ought not to be mistaken with our longing for the absolute on pain of the child bringing about the death of its parents, as Hegel asserts.

The aim of our union is not to procreate, because this would put its finality outside of itself, but to fulfil our longing for uniting with one another. And such a motion is not driven by a preconceived objective, which we ought to attain in some or other way but by its own necessity. This cannot for all that be satisfied at the expense of the elements that it intends to unite, on pain of being dashed. The motion and the elements that it attempts to unite are closely related to one another. Assuming such co-determination towards reaching the absolute makes our desire truly human.

And if any motion is determined by space and time, the one which results from desire is particularly complex. At first sight, it may seem that it is autonomous with regard to such coordinates, but this is not the case, at least if we aspire after a human sharing. And it is probably this apparent indeterminacy which led to the subjection of desire to supra-sensitive values on the one hand, and its falling back into mere instincts on the other hand. But, then, desire no longer exists—and, perhaps, no longer humanity either. Indeed, is it not desire that ensures our existence and our becoming as humans?

It is true that desire is identifiable with difficulty, and it is even more the case for its mutual sharing. From a spatial viewpoint, would it be possible to first suggest that the masculine desire seeks to take shelter in the feminine body? If this is the case, is it in search of a union with a woman or of a regression in the mother? The way of inhabiting the inner space of the feminine body is quite different according to such an alternative: if seeking a union can exist in the first case, the man is only in search of self-affection in the second case. And, at the level of interiority, what corresponds for a man to the fact of being in the body of a woman? Has not this question been eluded by speaking of penetration, on the one part, and of reproduction, on the other part? We have no word, no logos, to say to what experience and meaning being in a body other than our own corresponds.

Hence, blind drives or moral duties have been substituted for a sensitive experience of our fleshly intimacy. Almost nothing is said about the most irreducible event regarding our being as human. And is not our traditional logos—including the divine one—destined, even without our knowing, to be instilled into us in order that we should enter into communion with and through it to the detriment of uniting with one another thanks to our own desire?

On her side, how experiences a woman the fact of being inhabited by the man? Does she not often run the risk of splitting up into a more or less sensitive and merely physical experience and the excessive development of an imaginary world? An important part of her affects will also be transferred to the child, to her relations with the child. Also for her, alas!, a cultivation of sensitiveness is lacking, especially for passing to a shared sensitiveness without destroying herself or aspiring after mastering the other. In reality such a sharing needs to attain a transcendence with regard to sensitivity itself. Then the woman can welcome the other in herself, while respecting this other and herself as different. And this puts difference in her interiority as a comprehensive one—in that which can, perhaps, be called flesh. Indeed, it is no longer a question of a mere body but of a body which has also become psyche, soul and potentially word—in a way, logos. In such a body, a woman can from then on welcome another flesh and unite with it.

Such a union does not occur immediately. It calls for an elaboration of space and time from the part of the one and of the other. Because of the morphology of her body, the woman has probably a special role to assume in this process. Is she not more able than a man to perceive something about the being, and even the 'to be', of the other and to return to the other a living 'image', helping in this way this other to experience self-affection in the relation with her? This requires her to reach a perception of herself, one of a different nature from the self-consciousness to which Hegel alludes. Indeed, the issue here is not of a relation between her and herself as same or different, but of a relation in which the other as other takes part. However, this cannot lead the woman to lose the perception of herself on pain of becoming incapable of acknowledging the perception of the other as other. In her own flesh, the woman must ensure a sort of dialectical process between the 'to be' of the other and her own 'to be'. If nature itself in a way takes charge of this during the pregnancy, the placenta assuming the role of mediator between the mother and the foetus, the process which can ensure the mediation between her—and, furthermore, each of us—and the other in the amorous relationship, and in sexuate relationships in general, is too little taken into account. And yet, it is crucial for our becoming as humans.

Self-Affection and Self-Consciousness

By conceiving consciousness as supposedly universal and in the neuter, our tradition has prevented us from perceiving and cultivating a consciousness specific to the man, on the one hand, and to the woman, on the other hand. The mere idea that this might exist arouses scepticism and even irony. This amounts to ignoring that we then think that a consciousness in the masculine could correspond to any consciousness, to a consciousness presumed to be neutral and potentially universal. In this way we distort the truth of consciousness in general, but also that of the self-consciousness of man himself. Furthermore, paralyzed in a consciousness arbitrarily conceived as universal, energy that we invested in it splits into an abstract universality on the one hand and an instinctive naturalness on the other hand. From this result the misfortunes of our relational, especially of our amorous, life, which is consequently ruled by laws and absolutes imposed on us from an outside in a more or less arbitrary way regarding our natural belonging.

In order to define a self-consciousness which is more in accordance with the real and the truth, it would be advisable to start again from a sensitive self-affection, so preserving our natural energy and letting the particularities of each sexuate identity appear. Unveiling in this way the specific structure which underlies the self-consciousness of each allows us to conceive of a consciousness being in accordance with the truth of the real itself. We can hardly anticipate what this will modify in our manner of imagining truth and the logos. For example, it is not inconceivable that the process of reflection which underpins our cultural tradition, and as it is envisioned in Hegelian dialectics, only complies with the requirements of a masculine self-consciousness. As such, this process cannot assert that it is universal without harming both universality itself and masculine self-consciousness, then deprived of its specificity. There is no doubt that we can put an operation of our mind into the neuter in order to more easily reach universality. But of what universality is it then about? Can we speak of a self-consciousness in such a case? Or is the issue at stake rather conforming to a model of consciousness that is already mechanized or robotized by an extrapolation from life? However, the energy of the living being is used in order to ensure its functioning—at least it is the case in Hegelian dialectics, which entails a contradiction in his system that he did not overcome.

To solve such a contradiction, it is probably advisable to wonder about the sensitive element which plays a part in self-consciousness and to make it effective in a process more global than the one at work in Hegelian dialectics. It is thus a matter of acknowledging that sensitivity itself has a transcendental potential to which our self-affection, perceived as such, can aspire and lead.

Nevertheless, can one self alone ensure the dialectical process concerning affect(s)? Or does the latter need one self-affection to enter into relation with another self-affection, thus with another reality than an object, in order to remain sensitive? Indeed, how could we reduce the self-affection of the other as different from ourselves to an object that we could appropriate? Is it not hetero-affection that then must be at stake? And this makes the dialectical process really more complex! Because, if the drive which animates self-consciousness corresponds, according to Hegel, to a longing for one's self in search of this self through objects generating new desires, it is not the same at all regarding desire at a more global level. More precisely, limiting desire to such aspiration(s), as happens too often, runs the risk of depriving it of sensing the absolute after which it aspires. In reality desire aspires after a conjunction with another subject and not a self-achievement through the appropriation of object(s)—which can only represent a stage, a disappointing one in fact, of its quest. Must desire for all that be dependent on supra-sensitive ideals and absolutes or, instead, try to become embodied in relationship with another subject?

The duplication of the relation to object(s), which consciousness needs in order to return to itself, is then no longer possible—one subject cannot be duplicated by an other without being destroyed as subject. This does not mean that something of one does not take place and is not inscribed in the other, but appropriating it amounts for each to alienating its autonomy, thus its desire. Desire lasts as longing for the absolute only if the other resists any appropriation, either as an object or as a subject of desire; that is, if the transcendence of desire is preserved by both.

Then autonomy does not mean appropriating all the real by, to and for oneself but giving up appropriating what belongs to the life of the other, the latter being a human or a non-human being, and keeping faithfulness to oneself without aiming at being the one who one is not. This allows us to discover or return to the innocence—the dawn, as Nietzsche and Heidegger would probably say—of desire of the living being that we are.

Such an innocence cannot amount to a mere uncultured immediacy. Immediacy with regard to our desire for the absolute is not gained without a cultivation of our instincts or drives. It needs us to renounce 'objects' that we want impulsively to appropriate—which requires us to internalize energy itself. It is no longer a question of a sort of confrontation between a subject and object(s), between subjectivity and objectivity, but of the nature of the mediation itself. Will this be capable or not of allowing two subjects to enter into relation with one another, in particular a relation of desire, while preserving their longing for the absolute. The only mediation which is suitable for respecting the becoming of each is probably the one relative to our 'to be' itself, a 'to be' that sometimes we succeed in making happen in forming an ecstatic union with one another from the being that each is. Through this union both attempt to reach an impossible appropriation of their origin as a source of their desire.

The 'to be' for which we long, which we sometimes approach thanks to uniting with one another, does not result from a speculative elaboration—it is an appearing of our life mediated by desire thanks to our sexuate belonging. The external and internal differences, that the respect for our respective sexuate identity is able to maintain, grant us the possibility of transcending an undifferentiated flow of life while safeguarding the immediacy of life itself. Beyond the fact that it sends us back to our origin, sexuate belonging allows us, and even forces us, to assume our own life due to the perspective with which it provides us with regard to life in general and the abstract universality of human life. It gives to us both the freedom and the duty of mediating life in order to reproduce it, but firstly to cultivate it as human. When Aristotle says in *De Anima* that 'it is life that constitutes their being for the living' (Aristotle 1980–2011: 4,415 b 13), designating as life 'food, growth, and fading away by oneself' (ibid.: II, 1, 412–14), he misjudges—as other philosophers of the West will do after him—that desire is crucial for feeding life, contributing to its growth or causing its fading. Human life cannot be satisfied with the elements which exist in the universe for feeding itself, growing and even fading away; it needs desire of the other, meaning desire for and from the other, a desire which acts as a mediation between our natural and our cultural human belonging.

An Absolute Rooted in Nature

The desire for the other is also what can work as a mediation between individual and community. This mediation cannot be divided into a supposedly private mediation and a public mediation, but it must act at various levels of the relationship between individuals. This will allow amorous partners to behave in a civil manner and citizens to keep their natural particularity instead of becoming neutralized and abstract individuals.

The desire for the other also makes possible our not leaping from one to the multiple elements of a community of same ones but preserving and cultivating the relationship between two individuals, beginning with two individuals different by nature —hence the necessity of developing subjectivities which correspond to the natural identity of each.

This stage of a human culture, traces of which exist in the ancient Greek language, gradually has disappeared, which has led to an impoverishment and disembodiment of human subjectivity. And all the equalitarian claims, in particular on the part of women, are incapable of compensating for such a loss or of rectifying it. They do not relate to that which is really at stake: a lack of acknowledgement of the existence of two identities, not only at the natural level but also at the cultural level.

To succeed in such an undertaking, we must overcome the logical dualism which underlies our culture, especially the one between the inner and the external self, notably with regard to our relations to the absolute. Once more, sexuate identity provides us with a structure which can mediate between the traditional terms of such an opposition, including when they are expressed as idealism and realism.

As sexuate, our desire aims at the absolute, but our tradition cut it off from its natural determination(s) by subjecting it to an absolute presumed to be real because it is situated outside of our original self—as well as the absolute as the means to reach it or the prohibitions imposed on our longings. And yet, we long for the absolute in a way determined by what or who we are—in a way by a 'within us'—which aspires after an absolute situated both within and outside us. Thus we long for the absolute, but this longing can be fulfilled only through an amorous union with an other. Sexuate desire overcomes the traditional opposition between realism and idealism; that is, between an objectivity, which is unconcerned about our subjectivity, and the aspirations arising from our internal being alone. It depends on a structuring of our being which is neither merely objective nor merely subjective and which joins together our inner self to our external self.

This not only objective but also subjective structure, which determines objectively our subjectivity, has been too little taken into account. And it is not thoughtless to wonder whether such oversight is not the cause of the power of the technique on the real and on our subjectivity. For lack of acknowledging the physical-psychical structure which intervenes between ourselves and the world, we have created a mechanism external to ourselves which in a way substitutes for this structure, beginning with the logos itself.

Hence, we mistake a projection of our sensations, affects and aspirations onto the world for objectivity, whereas it is a part of our subjectivity that we do not recognize as such. This is particularly true about the absolute, which obviously does not exist objectively apart from a subjective production. From this viewpoint, it is interesting to note all the dogmatic attempts which argue about the objective existence of an absolute which corresponds with a secret necessity of our subjectivity. It is also fruitful to observe in this connection that idealism dwells a lot on what is probably an immediate natural experience, which is put on hold by supra-sensitive ideals, for lack of having acknowledged and cultivated it in an adequate way, especially as desire.

In reality, aspiring after the absolute exists in us as soon as we are capable of distancing ourselves from an immediate experience. But our culture has not taken into account enough this part of us which, more than any other, longs for the absolute and needs the means to be expressed and developed. Instead of our path towards the absolute being mapped out by moral imperatives, it is our incarnation, with its potential and its limits, which ought to act as a framework for our passage from a natural immediate experience to an experience of the absolute able to correspond with the former. And this would permit us to reconcile nature and the divine which, in reality, take part in the same experience of the real.

In this way, the opposition between the divine, as the infinite existing in the presumed finiteness of nature, and the divine, which would be distinct from nature and brought into it by a divine will, can be overcome—which can amount to surmounting the opposition between a certain conception of Christianity on the one hand, and paganism on the other hand ('De la relation entre la philosophie de la nature et la philosophie en général', F.W.J. Schelling or G.W.F. Hegel, dans *La différence entre les systèmes philosophiques de Fichte et de Schelling*, Hegel 1986: p. 212). Our sexuate belonging, although it is innate, can be spiritualized by desire and unites with another sexuate belonging to freely reach the absolute. Already in each of us the infinite can be experienced and contemplated in finiteness thanks to desire, and the opposition between what is innate and what is acquired can, then, be overcome. However, the union between two different desires makes us reach another stage, and even a new era, with regard to the relation between nature and the divine. Indeed, two infinites, which potentially exist but are embodied in the finiteness of each, unite with one another thanks to an at least relative freedom. This means that the opposition between the innate infinite and the infinite separate from nature, which would characterize the difference between paganism and monotheism, is overcome.

Through desire, the infinite comes into the finiteness of a natural existence, but it also projects itself onto another natural existence, in which it is in search of its absolute fulfilment. Human being itself in this way can contribute to the presence of the infinite in the finite, so opening the time of another relation between nature and the divine. Humans can generate the divine between themselves by uniting with one another as natural beings who are transformed by their longing for the infinite. Each of us can this way return to the other not only their image, but the experience of the absolute that he or she lives through and, as for them, awakens in the other.

Sometimes we can reach a union through a common longing for the absolute, but this can happen only if we keep our difference(s) and preserve the pureness of the energy which unites us. If the faithfulness to nature and the respect for morality have traditionally been considered to be opposite attitudes, they are now combined with one another towards our experiencing the absolute. This absolute cannot exist without a participation of nature, about which the respect for the specific incarnation of each needs a moral, or rather an ethical, concern—which introduces us into a rational order without either dogmatism or quibbling of understanding.

The division into nature and spirit, with its consequent dichotomies, can be surmounted by acknowledging that one does not exist without the other, but that it is their co-belonging which allows them to elevate one another to a transcendental level. Hence, our soul has not to gain a virginity capable of thinking by freeing itself from any material tie but to preserve the breath, of which it is made up, from being used for merely empirical requirements. Hence also the particular can be incorporated into the universal through cultivating our breathing and reaching our being in communion through it.

Light for Which Sensitivity Longs

Being in communion with one another calls for our breath being incarnate—which cannot occur without a cultivation of our sensitivity that the duality of subjectivities permits. The becoming of spirit then no longer happens through a tearing into two of reason but through a meeting between two irreducibly different subjectivities. This, finally, can absolve each one from being both living and an other for oneself. Indeed, our consideration for an insurmountable otherness liberates us from this other which accompanied us as living, one could say from our shadow, and, therefore, makes unlimited the absolute corresponding to each particular being. It is between two different living beings that reason makes its way towards the absolute, an absolute the limit of which henceforth vanishes endlessly. This limit has been acknowledged and assumed as the tearing of human being itself into two parts, and it has no longer to be projected onto reason or the absolute. It exists and is insuperable, but it is this limit which makes possible our having access to an indefinitely open absolute.

In order that such an absolute should remain living, and thus in becoming, it is important that each, at every time, takes on its partiality, especially as a sensitive body. Each one must consent to the other passively, welcome the carnal presence of the other, including in oneself, not for appropriating it but for giving this other back to itself while remembering it towards a union between two different beings.

The duality of natures and consciousnesses can make obsolete the necessity of dichotomies for our understanding. The natural delimitation between two subjectivities means that the absolute no longer has to overcome limitations created by spirit. The absolute arises from a desire of our nature to live it in uniting with an/its other human, which cannot be achieved without the help of consciousness as self-consciousness. This one has not to extricate itself from a totality, it is at once partial, a thing that it can realize through its specific self-affection. Consciousness then remains sensitive, and it does not become merely speculative; which allows it to be faithful to an original experience of life as an absolute with a view towards its cultivation.

Consciousness takes on the non-being of its particular sexuate belonging as that which preserves its aiming at a living absolute as a possibility for it. What is more, by assuming its particularity, consciousness at the same time expels a negative outside of itself. Thus reaching a self-consciousness appropriate to ourselves happens by our agreeing not to be the consciousness of the other. And such self-consciousness now corresponds with a specific nature which can be subjected to a dialectical process without separating form from matter in an absolute way.

Indeed, its limits are not determined by understanding but by nature itself endeavouring to become spiritual as such.

It is, then, up to the absolute to take into account a natural determination; something that, by the way, it has always done but without knowing it, at least consciously. Indeed, has not considering our sensitivity to be doomed to finiteness and our intellect fit for the infinite subjected our conception of the absolute to the traditional requirements of a masculine consciousness unaware of its determination(s)? But does not that which happens in our culture today show the limit of this conception of the absolute? And is not this limit due to favouring intellect to the detriment of sensitivity? Is it not advisable to consider the infinite of which sensitivity itself is capable, the infinite after which it aspires, before letting understanding decide on the nature of the absolute—which it cannot do only by itself because it is desire which aims at the absolute? How can intellect claim the right to decide on the absolute and pretend that it alone holds light when it does not take into account the light that desire senses, the light that desire itself already is? Does not speculation then lead us to a more impenetrable night than the one which would correspond with desire? Because the latter is not necessarily blind, but it trusts touch more than sight, and our culture leads it astray by a logic of sameness and an emphasis placed on a plurality of objects through which it loses its most original source.

Hence, desire enters into a universe of opposites, of dichotomies, of violences and concessions which pervert our natural energy and leave us unsatisfied. Desire arises from an original difference that all opposites and dichotomies cover, hiding the light of sensitivity in a maze of rationalizations of understanding which end in nothing, and which compensate for this nothingness with the faith in something or someone. In this way understanding saves the status of the object by making it irrefutable by the subject.

Before giving ourselves up to faith it would be advisable for us to experience what absolute can be generated by the conjunction of two longings for the absolute which are determined by different natural belongings. Such an absolute is not reached through overcoming opposites but through a union in difference. And it is no longer necessary to 'intensify a division into two in order to increase the need for uniting in a totality', as Hegel maintains, because the division in two exists and it is insuperable; we have just to respect it. Besides, this division naturally longs for a union. And such a union, instead of calling for an elimination, requires us to give up believing in something that is not true: the fact that object(s) would be capable of corresponding with our longing for the absolute. It is thus a matter of renouncing an erroneous investment to turn our desire towards another subject instead of towards objects. Then our spirit is already prepared for having a respectful relationship with a subject naturally different from us, and this relation is the only one which is able to cultivate sensitive immediacy while safeguarding both the immediacy and the sensitivity of our longing.

What is more, our desire aims at a union—in Hegelian terms at a synthesis—which calls for an opening and not a closing of the 'system' or the totality. Desire prompts us to open up to the other, and not to conflict with the other; which allows us to unite with one another towards an absolute which itself remains potentially open. If this can happen, it is because sexuate difference consists both of matter(s) and of form(s), without amounting to a contrast between matter and form(s), as is generally presupposed. The two sexes are suppliers of matter and form(s), and it is the fact that they are different, but not opposite, which contributes to making them autonomous with respect to each other. If they unite with one another it is with the aim of reaching another absolute, a still more absolute absolute, the objectivity of which is irreducible to any object, and is the fruit of a conjunction between two different subjectivities.

Such a conjunction can be achieved only thanks to a natural energy aspiring after the absolute. The shape that this absolute can take can be called into question in order to improve the nature of the absolute itself, not necessarily in a quantitative way but in a qualitative way, especially with regard to a correspondence with the 'to be' that each human must incarnate and its always ongoing becoming or genesis. The latter cannot be determined a priori and carried out only through an adequacy between subject and object(s). It is between two subjects that the human 'to be' can be generated thanks to a suitable conjunction in difference, which above all depends on the quality of energy which allows them to relate to and unite with one another.

Such quality implies that matter and form(s) no longer conflict with each other, with the need for a continuous suppression of one by the other. Henceforth, one transforms the other by a sort of embrace and, in such a transformation, form is more a means or a mediation than an objective or an end. In this way our desire takes shape from the matter from which it arises and towards the matter at which it aims. However, any of these matters is undetermined or inert. Desire aims at uniting them, acting as a mediation between two different matters. One could say that what drives it is a transcendental intuition in which desire assembles matter and consciousness, reality and ideality, immanence and transcendence.

Desire as Transcendental Intuition

Going back to our sexuate desire reverses the trend of our culture which mistakes idea for the real, or subjects matter to consciousness. Such a gesture returns desire to its living origin in which physical nature and form(s) already interact. Instead of subjecting an undetermined, and supposedly neuter, aspiration to forms which turn it towards the absolute, the determined nature of our longing is then cultivated as such, because in it lies the absolute at which our desire aims. This cultivation must originate from it as a living sap, which tries to blossom in faithfulness to the matter that it makes blossom.

Desire, as a transcendental intuition, senses that, for it, the path towards the absolute can be cleared through the other, an other who would be able to correspond with such intuition. However, instead of searching for transcendence beyond matter, desire aspires after finding transcendence in matter itself, a matter with which it could combine to soothe its thirst for the absolute. At least it is so a first time, at a stage in which the risk of transforming the other into an object exists. But this would amount to falling again into the subject–object, subjectivity–objectivity, and even idea–real dichotomies. In this case, desire falls back into the trap of a master–slave struggle which deprives it of a living relation to the absolute. More exactly and radically, it is facing an insoluble dilemma: to long for matter or spirit, object or subject, real or idea. And our longing for the absolute thus gets lost in such alternatives.

That which keeps us faithful to the real while continuing to aspire after transcendence is our longing for uniting with an other as other, firstly an other naturally different from us. Through such a desire, human being aims at its spiritual accomplishment in faithfulness to its nature. In order to unite with the other, it unites in itself the body with soul and spirit, and so it makes its body spiritual. In other words, it transforms the materiality of its body into flesh.

Desire attempts to unite with the other not by overcoming opposites, which result from a certain logic, but by its aiming at our becoming, more precisely at transforming its physical background into a spiritual background. Then our desire for the other becomes an aspiration after uniting with this other; that is, our longing moves from a term of the relation to the relation itself, a relation which exists thanks to an insuperable difference. If it succeeds in preserving this difference, without the latter being reduced to an opposition between the two terms or one of them being reduced to an object, this relation is by itself spiritual. Such a spiritual quality results from a respect for life in its various embodiments.

For Hegel, there is no development of thought without intuition. However, this intuition is continually contradicted by reflection which objects to it. Aiming at the absolute then requires us to overcome the antinomy between intuition and reflection. Such a dialectical process can take place only inside an already constructed world.

Indeed, if I return to the living world, I note that there is not a real opposition between myself and another living being. When I adopt the dialectical method of Hegel, I cut myself off from my living belonging and from an effective relationship with another living being. And yet, there is no antinomy between me and another living being, and the question is thus: How can I carry out my becoming without such an antinomy because there is not a mere continuity between us either? It is then a matter of discovering another method in which intuition cannot be refuted by reasoning.

Perhaps we must give up using the word intuition with its past meaning: to apprehend by sight with a presentiment of what is not yet appearing. We must return into our deeper and more comprehensive sensitivity or flesh, and even adopt another word or, at least, modify its meaning. Why not use 'sensing', but as what can happen through being touched? The dialectical process which is needed by such a touch perception is different from the Hegelian one. Indeed, a tactile experience can exist between two living beings, especially between two humans, and it is probably that which gives rise to desire. The becoming of this sensitive experience towards the absolute no longer results from an opposition between what I experience and the existence of the other but through the difference between what I experience of the other and what this other experiences. There is no antinomy between the two: what I experience of the other cannot be the opposite of what he or she experiences if we are both faithful to the living being that we are. And, if in order to become the one who I am and to contribute to the becoming of our relation I must take on the fact that I am not the other, this does not mean that I do not perceive anything of the one who he or she is. However, in order to acknowledge this I must assume the fact that I am not completely them.

I could say, differently from the words which sometimes are uttered in a mystical discourse: I am you on the condition of not being you. And this occurs at a double or triple level. I am not you as being, either originally or currently, if you have grown in faithfulness to your own 'to be'. Nevertheless, I can sometimes experience better than you the 'to be' that you are, which allows me to give birth to you at an ontological level. An inner dwelling place in my flesh makes this bringing you, or bringing you again, into the world possible, provided that I assume our difference. If, at the mental level, the absolute can correspond to an idea or an ideal, at a comprehensive level, longing for the absolute makes perhaps possible for us to incarnate our 'to be' and that of the other as different towards our uniting with one another.

The limit and interval between these two different 'to be' are what enable us to open up to the absolute without even resorting to understanding and reasoning. Then it is no longer a matter of overcoming opposites defined by our understanding, which is unable to speculate otherwise, but of us taking on a difference between two absolutes and so opening up to an absolute which is still more absolute. The absolute at which each of us is capable of aiming allows us to structure a world, notably of thinking, but this world can be surpassed towards a horizon which opens up to a more absolute absolute by harmonizing with, instead of opposing, another absolute. The particularity of these worlds or horizons—Hegel probably would say of these systems—is that they remain open. In this way, they are both structured and faithful to the living being that we are. They are determined by our own specific belonging and its opening up to relating to the other as naturally different.

The way of evolving of these 'systems' or worlds is more qualitative than quantitative. It does not correspond to the extension or expansion of a system or a world but to a qualitative change, which becomes obvious notably through the density of energy allowing each to gain a more suitable relation to the transcendental and a relationship between two of a more transcendental nature too. Thus empirical and transcendental no longer conflict with one another but they attempt to be in accordance with one another in order to reach an absolute in which subjective and objective gradually end in being the same.

There is not for all that any object at stake because neither the other nor myself are reducible to an object. And it is no longer the relation between subject and object(s) which is in search of appropriation, equality or identity. Each subjectivity is in search of itself as well as in a relation to itself as in a relation to the other, but this search develops through a process of self-affection extraneous to the subject–object relation. Such a process makes possible a more comprehensive and fulfilled becoming for each and for the relationship with the other. The issue is that this becoming cannot be interrupted by an appropriation of the process by either of them. Affection and self-affection must remain what acts as an invisible dwelling, both internal and external, in which each stays and preserves an integrity which allows it to become itself and to enter into a relationship with the other with respect for the two subjectivities. Such a process is really complex because it is not easy to distinguish in one's affect(s) and even self-affection what belongs truly to oneself and what belongs to the other.

This, furthermore, raises a question about the nature of consciousness itself, especially of self-consciousness. How can we affirm that it is really 'pure' and that the other does not participate in it? However, the consciousness of the other affects us differently from the consciousness of an object—we cannot distance and differentiate ourselves from him or her as we can do from an object. Contrasting subject with object(s) is not possible when it is a question of the other and ourselves, and this subject–subject relationship needs another logic. Our tradition did not care about this need and it implicitly left this concern to the religious field, which led to a cultural aporia with regard to relating to one another.

The other alters my consciousness and it is not by making myself an object for myself that I can free myself from this alteration. The latter happens before such a process, which by the way could be only reactive. Besides, the relation to and with the other is never merely empirical and I cannot contrast it with a relation to the transcendental. The other, when it is considered to be truly other, is transcendent to me, and this transcendence is both natural and spiritual. It is such a relation which is able to make my consciousness virgin again with regard to an unconscious alteration which is, at least partially, due to the other.

Thinking about the nature of our 'to be' can also contribute to liberating our consciousness from what unconsciously affects it. Our way of thinking of being is based on an 'it is', which already presupposes an 'I am' who asserted it, but it is not possible to reduce 'you are' to an 'it is' and even 'he is' or 'she is'. 'You are' takes place between an 'I am', which one way or another remains faithful to my nature and expresses my 'to be' as a life of my own, and an 'it is' which, at least traditionally, is situated and viewed inside a system of representations which already has removed being from a living existence.

5

Sketch of a Logic of Intersubjectivity

From Subject–Object Adequacy to Subject–Subject Connection

The union between the man and the woman differs from a synthesis. It is not a question of opposite elements, which become reconciled with one another in order to compose a unity, but of two human beings, which appeal to one another in order to become more than one—to generate an additional 'to be' in comparison with what or whom they already are. In the first case, the two elements are moved by a dynamism which is not really their own but results from their definition as opposites. In the second case, the dynamism is produced by the living beings that they are, the difference of which is capable of giving birth to a new being not only at the natural level but also at the spiritual or ontological level. The one, the other and their union represent three potential absolutes which engender one another.

The union between a man and a woman does not aim at the reconciliation of two opposite parts of a human being but at the production of a new being that we too often imagine can only be a natural one. In reality, through their union, the man and the woman are, or ought

© The Author(s) 2019
L. Irigaray, *Sharing the Fire*,
https://doi.org/10.1007/978-3-030-28330-8_5

to be, at the same time engendered, created and spiritualized one and the other and by one another. The fact that such a union, which would be faithful to the potential of the real itself, has been underrated in its ontological fruitfulness is the cause of an additional imagination, which led to a split between reality and ideality and a lack of recognition of what this union really is. From such a misapprehension many other oppositions arose, amongst which was that between materialism and idealism.

In order that the union between a man and a woman should become truly effective, each consciousness must become a true self-consciousness. But, henceforth, it is in the name of reality and not of ideality that this process is needed. Instead of depending on, and thus being subordinate to, object(s), the real then depends on our desire for a con-junction with another subject. In our past cultural, especially philosophical, tradition, consciousness set it up by itself but received its determination(s)—in a way its content(s)—from its relation to object(s) that it opposed in order to appear to itself as such. Now, consciousness is considered to be determined in itself, notably through the background from which it springs, in particular its sexuate belonging. It no longer needs opposing object(s) to define itself as consciousness. It evades this contradiction, but it must undertake another process to become effective.

Consciousness is not immediately aware of its own determination(s). It is only indirectly that such determination(s) can appear to it, as well as through observing particularities in the way of behaving of the self and the manner in which subjectivity expresses itself as through noting difference(s) in relation to those of the other. So becoming objective for itself, the determination(s) of consciousness allows it to exist and to become what it is without opposing itself, even unconsciously.

Consciousness must come to terms with another consciousness, especially the one of the subject for which it longs, as a way to reach the absolute. Then, again, it is not a question of our reducing the other to an object without risking thwarting the search for the absolute that this other as other embodies for us. In reality, the dependence of the subject upon object(s) already amounts to a sort of limitation of its potential in order to maintain its becoming towards the absolute. Resorting to object(s) is of use for specifying a finiteness which, in fact, already exists in consciousness itself as determined. Ignoring the original and natural determination(s) of consciousness, the philosopher, and more generally any subject, is forced to impose on it artificial limits, from which it vainly will attempt to free itself by opposing them. Our consciousness is trapped within the circle that it, itself, has created for producing itself as limited. And yet, acknowledging it as being the one that it was—that is, determined—was sufficient.

For lack of admitting that it is determined, consciousness, which then claims that it is only ideal, is no more than a human production, the physical nature of which is unrecognized. Indeed, who could affirm that the syntax of one's discourse is extraneous to the forms and the structure of one's body? What would happen, in this case, between the time when one speaks and the time when one lives? How and why did our culture make such a cut between the two? And what results from this cut with regard to truth itself?

Will we then bring forward the fact that consciousness must enjoy freedom? What freedom is it about? Is it other than an abstract energy which comes from a lack of incarnation and is of use for the functioning of a mechanism cut off from life? Does not freedom, instead, consist in the possibility of becoming who I am? And is it not by taking the risk of longing for you that I liberate, and even produce, my freedom?

Whereas others exhaust themselves in the search for a synthesis between subject and object, idealism and realism, intuition and duty, do I not succeed in overcoming—or avoiding—such dichotomies thanks to my desire for you? Does not this desire, which springs from my flesh and aspires after uniting with yours, exist beyond such dilemmas? Which certainly results from its nature, but also from the energy which drives it. And this happens naturally without any speculative effort.

Reason must endeavour not to harm the natural belonging of desire. Instead of removing desire from its physical origin, of cutting it off from flesh, the task of reason ought to contribute to its union with a desire which is different. And yet, a logic making possible such a union is still lacking. Before imposing limits on our desire, reason must carry out its own transformation. Instead of maintaining that it is capable of controlling subjectivity, reason ought to admit that our identity is first natural and that it has to negotiate with this reality. Then, reason will perceive that a human consciousness is both physically determined and animated by a desire for the absolute. Some philosophies allocate to the object that which is already part of our subjectivity, and the split of the latter into subject and object is thus useless for bringing us back to the real and the infinite. Sexuate belonging makes our subjectivity able to correspond with both, and it also assigns to subjectivity an objectivity which can exist and express itself without any object. Our specificity in comparison with a subject naturally different, which appears notably through our respective acts and works, is able to reveal to us what or who we are. There is thus no need, for us, to resort to object(s) extraneous to our subjectivity in order that this one should exist, all the more so since this would bring about an infinite production of mutual delimitations between subject and object(s). The objectivity of our subjectivity appears through the form(s) and the structure which are expressed by our faithfulness to our own nature.

Hence, nature itself no longer leads us to experience the absolute, the infinite or eternity in a way that is too subjective. Indeed, experiencing our own natural belonging, especially thanks to its difference in comparison with the one of the other, gives back an objectivity to our perceptions—and it is the same with our instincts or feelings. The opposition between subject and object remains effective only when we exclude the other from what we experience, or when we reduce our affects to a stage of our development that we must overcome in order to fulfil our longing for the absolute, instead of considering them to be a path towards the absolute.

As for the opposition between necessity and liberty, it lasts above all when we neglect the fact that we are relational beings and we cannot accomplish ourselves without taking into account our relation to and with the world, all the living beings which populate it, and especially to and with the other(s) different from ourselves by nature. In other words, realizing our potential requires us to develop in accordance with our necessities, and to become the ones who we are, as Nietzsche would say. For such a becoming he (alas!) underestimated the relational part of his being and founded his will to power in a too partial and ideal way with regard to his necessities, in particular those relative to dynamism and energy. He did not assess and place his limits so that he could keep alive the source of his becoming. He focused too much on what he opposed and which destroyed him without cultivating sufficiently what might have allowed him to grow by transforming himself. He also paid too great importance to his nature as a mere physiology without considering sufficiently the role and the impact of his sexuate belonging. For lack of taking into account such determination and energy potential Nietzsche little by little exhausted himself.

Nature and Freedom

Those who substitute concepts for the dynamism that life brings destroy their own potential. They consider our natural determination to be a limitation, in particular because death, without realizing that the source of the motion towards transcending themselves, notably through desire, lies in it. In nature itself is the origin of our freedom with regard to both our own growing and our opening up to the world, especially to the other. Thus contrasting nature with freedom does not make sense.

Moreover, such a gesture locks our subjectivity in a circle of which it is almost impossible for it to go out. Indeed what a philosopher, and more generally our culture, call freedom—a freedom in the name of which we intervene in nature—is often a mere unconscious way of imitating nature, a nature of which we have not interpreted the intervention in our manner of thinking and even of existing. Consequently, we imagine that we impose on nature measures which already amount to determination(s) that it has imposed on us without us knowing. How could we emerge from such a blind circularity? This can happen only by acknowledging and assuming how much we are determined by nature and the fact that our existence entails our incarnating such natural determination.

Contrasting our natural belonging with freedom, as many Western philosophers did, also amounts to considering our freedom to be something external to us and not our capability of achieving the being that we are. To be free, then, would mean opposing our being more than accomplishing it. Indeed, such a behaviour splits us into two irreconcilable parts instead of leading them to contribute towards our fulfilment.

We are not made up of a modifiable matter and of a freedom which would fit reason. Matter of which we consist, our flesh, is already potentially rational, and it is up to us to acquire the freedom of living it as such; which asks us to make certain choices, especially qualitative and not quantitative ones, which contribute towards the becoming of our comprehensive being without subjecting it to laws extraneous to life.

Such laws thwart our growing and, moreover, by intending to subdue nature, 'they destroy any mutual relationships which are really free, any relation which is infinite for itself, which is without limits and thus beautiful', as Hegel writes (in *La différence entre les systèmes philosophiques de Fichte et de Schelling*, p. 157/ *The Difference between Fichte's and Schelling's System of Philosophy*, p. 144, Hegel 1986, my translation). They give rise only to a tyrannical community whereas when the freedom of everyone is dependent on one's own nature, a community of living beings can exist. And it is all the more so since nature involves a being in relation(s) which both determines the individual becoming and connects it with the becoming of the other in a living and concrete way, as is or ought to be the case with sexuation. Our becoming implies that we transcend ourselves through relationships with the naturally different other, while taking into account and respecting this difference towards making possible a living community.

Such a community is henceforth structured by desire more than by laws or concepts extraneous to life. And caring about the other amounts to taking care of ourselves because the desire for/of the other is necessary for our own becoming. If we do not respect and care about the other as other, we thwart our own relation to the absolute. Thus laws extraneous to nature are not those which can truly form a community, whereas the consideration for the relational requirements that our nature entails can contribute towards that. Laws as well as morality ought to be concerned about the preservation of such imperatives. When they neglect this care, they lead citizens to their being torn in themselves and between themselves, between a matter deprived of forms and formal concepts or rights unsuitable for a physical belonging. This gives rise to a state which imposes itself as an abstract and despotic mechanism upon citizens who are no more than atoms without life or identity of their own, especially at the relational level, and are thus unable to form a community of living beings (cf. ibid.: pp. 161–162/ pp. 148–149). Their instincts and drives are repressed, and even punished by rights and laws instead of being acknowledged and cultivated as that which can provide living links for the members of a community. Laws and morality are then what are intended to give forms to a matter which is presupposed to be without forms and vitality of its own.

In reality, sexuation acts as that which can overcome, or rather avoid, the opposition between a 'natural diversity' incapable of unifying itself and a formal identity laid down from the outside. The self-determination that sexuation entails does not grant us an arbitrary freedom, which could claim the right to intervene in the natural belonging of the other, of others; this self-determination is firstly one which depends on one's own nature. Then desire of the other—as desire for or from the other—is not only what allows us to become aware of our sexuate belonging but also what incites us to take care of the other as of the one who participates as other in our own accomplishment. Rights and morality must contribute towards the fulfilment of our longings instead of repressing or chastising what remains alive in us.

As long as we are living and respectful of our difference(s), we preserve between us a space in which we can live and a space in which we can build, whereas the opposition between us, beyond the fact that it paralyzes or destroys what attracts us to one another, artificially empties the space. Our frustrations and remainders of instincts, which are often transformed into a will to dominate or to submit, even at the level of culture and community, then fill such a space with cries and groaning, but also with various claims, conflicts and debates which are both useless and in a way artificial, as the opposition between us itself is.

On the contrary, the space that the difference between us opens can be a place in which the strength and fullness of our desire can be expressed, a place in which it can receive content and take form in its search for uniting with another desire. The link of freedom with necessity, that our desire wants to reach and tries to offer to the other as a sharing of life, is already a work of art because it allows us to unify in ourselves vital and ideal aspirations. Furthermore, recognizing the other as other delimits the transcendental framework inside which desire can become incarnate; which in a way makes useless any moral duty. The respect for the other, that my desire needs for lasting, already transforms my longing so that it could express itself in community without becoming cut off from my own interiority, or the latter being itself split. What is more, this transcendental frame brings a certain objectivity to my desire and permits me to shape it by myself without laws, extraneous to it, having to care about that.

Crucial Stage of the Relation Between Two

When it tries to overcome our subjective split into two, Western philosophy attempts to overcome what it traditionally brought about. Indeed, it itself has created such a division for lack of taking into account the fact that humanity is comprised of two parts. Moreover, it endeavours to reach a real that it has already elaborated instead of starting from the existing real. Hence, endless debates occur about what is real and what is ideal, even though both are already linked in each of us, as we have to deal with the longing for the absolute which arises in us. At least, it ought to be so if the nature of the relation between us was considered to be a difference, but not an opposition in which one must be abolished in order that the other should rise to the infinite. Which makes their union—or synthesis, in Hegelian terms—impossible while keeping them dependent on one another.

By acknowledging that the two parts of humanity have the same value in nature but are different as identities, without being for all that opposites that could be integrated into a higher unity, philosophy can open up the horizon of a new logic founded on a relationship between two different subjects, and not on the traditional subject–object relation. Indeed, the subjects are different by nature and not only defined as such by some or other consciousness, and they cannot abolish one another because their longing for the absolute is a longing for their meeting— not in the name of an absolute considered objective and universal but towards the union of their natural and transcendental longing for the absolute. Their difference has not to be reduced in the search for the absolute, as is the case for a constructed opposition. It is this difference which supports the unity of each identity and the longing of each for transcending itself thanks to the existence of another identity, irreducible to its own.

The difference between these identities is no longer merely constructed and dependent on some or other idea, ideal or ideology, it is also real—and as such it is qualitative and not only quantitative. It is not a more or less of this or that, for example of matter or form, which, then, defines difference; rather, it is a question of a material and ideal— or *idéel*—difference in the relation to the absolute. The difference between two differently sexuated subjects must be considered in this way as far as the becoming of each, but also the possibility of a union between the two, is concerned. The fact of having reduced this difference to a difference between two opposite polarities has prevented this union from happening both at a natural and a spiritual level, depriving the two subjectivities of their longing for the absolute in each other and through each other.

When this union occurs, it frees matter as living from already constructed forms and returns it, transformed, to a potentially transcendental level, from which each is then given to itself as human and the horizon in which humanity can be born and develop as such is delimited. It is no longer in the same absolute that elements, presumed to be opposite, can and must unite with each other, and thus the absolute is no longer in a way determined a priori either. Through the union between two naturally different identities, the absolute itself receives new matter and configuration. It is up to each one to contribute to the qualitative nature of such an absolute, so that it could give rise to both a more accomplished humanity and more responsible relations between all the living beings. Indeed, the fecundity of this absolute does not confine itself to the becoming of those who take the risk of uniting with one another in order to found a new life and a new world. Its fruitfulness spreads out over others and over the world, yet without being able to correspond with the same sort of sharing.

Only between two living beings, the body itself as matter can be the source and the place of our sharing. And, between the two, the subject–object syntactic connection is no longer the one which is suitable for favouring a link between nature and spirit. Each is both nature and spirit, and no object is necessary between them if they recognize each other as such without dividing themselves into a body and a mind. Between them as two, each subjectivity corresponds with a body which can unite with the other and find in this union the source and the becoming which fit a desire for the absolute. The mediation of an object is not necessary between two living beings, especially two subjects sexually different by nature.

Nevertheless, such mediation is necessary at the level of a community, above all if this one is based on sameness, identity and equality regardless of the diversity which composes the natural order. Such variety can be really taken into account only by a subjectivity which is concerned with its difference in relation to another subjectivity. Otherwise, the natural diversity might fall again into a subject-object logic, whatever the autonomy and quasi-subjectivity which are attributed to the living beings which make it up. To overcome the subject–object predicative logic, a relationship between two naturally different subjects is crucial. Only in such a meeting and a union can a body and a soul unite with each other and the copula—to be—be of use not merely in the search for the absolute by a single subject through relating to object(s), but in the longing for the absolute that the conjunction between two naturally different subjects can arouse.

The nature of such an absolute is quite different. In a solitary aspiration after the absolute, subjectivity runs the risk of exhausting the real that it represents in its search for shapes and forms or of splitting up into a multiplicity of objects into which it invests itself. And this happens when subjectivity does not solve in itself the connection of its transcendental longing with its natural origin. This cannot be achieved by passing from a personal natural belonging to a community belonging, neglecting the stage of the cultivation of the relationship with a subjectivity differently structured, notably by its sexuation. Only this kind of situation allows us to combine nature with intellect, necessity with liberty, to reach the absolute. It only allows us to overcome the dichotomy between interiority and exteriority through dealing with two different interiorities, the becoming of which is together supported and limited by one another.

This becoming is both real or physical and spiritual. And Hegel would probably agree with me that desire then acts as a light which enlivens the gravity of the bodies in order to make them ascend and be attracted to each other in a way that remains physical, but a physical endowed with different properties which are able to restore or awaken in our soma a motion in which freedom and thinking can have a share.

Hegel would also maintain that for the living being, or the 'animal', that we are, light must be both external and internal. He even asserts that 'in the animal, light then exists by itself as both subjective and objective because of the polarity of the sexes; each individual searches for itself and finds itself in an other. Light remains internalized with a greater intensity in the animal, in which it establishes individuality, like a more or less variable voice, like a subjectivity in a state of general communication, which recognizes itself and wants to be recognized' (*La différence entre les systèmes philosophiques de Fichte et de Schelling*, p. 179/*The Difference between the Fichte's and Schelling's System of Philosophy*, p. 168, Hegel 1986, my translation).

Unfortunately, Hegel does not consider sufficiently what happens in a union between two naturally different humans in which both matter and spirit, nature and mind, take part. Even if, without lingering much on that, he seems to give up a dichotomy between the genuses, his dialectical process does not involve the possibility of a transformation of the physical matter by the light of desire, and he opts for the ideal— or the *idéel*—and the common without taking enough into account the real, dynamic and spiritual fruitfulness of the carnal relations between the sexes. This remains a link which is too little broached in his thought even if it seems that he wanted to treat of it.

Hence, Hegel contrasts consciousness with nature in a way that a consciousness dependent on a theoretical construction needs more than nature itself. In reality, the oppositions that his dialectics intends to overcome are problematic oppositions because the two elements, which are presumed to be opposite, have not the same value, and the one which prevails over the other is not autonomous with respect to this other. Contrasting elements in order to overcome their opposition thus seems to be a strategy for entrusting to the mind and not to nature the development of the dialectical process.

Sharing the Fire

One symptom among many others bearing witness to the subjection of matter to spirit is the fact that Hegel, although he takes an interest in the physical properties, goes from gravity to light without lingering on the question of fire. And yet, it is fire which acts as a possible transition from the natural to the spiritual state, especially through the mediation of desire. The intervention of heat as a stage of the evolution of matter is nevertheless tackled in *The Encyclopedia of the Philosophical Sciences in Basic Outline* (Hegel 1970/2010: §287–290). But heat is viewed in terms of its negative effects—loss of the limits of the bodies, alteration of gravity and cohesion, lack of qualities—more than in its positive contribution to the growth, the attraction, the transformation of the bodies. This seems to result from the insufficient attention that Hegel attaches to desire.

There is no doubt that fire, including the fire of desire, blurs the already existing limits, but this can give rise to new limits. It is the same when desire affects a merely physical cohesion in order to produce one which is more spiritual. And if desire can act in this way, does this not mean that it involves motion and heat? Certainly some light arouses desire, but the impact of the latter on matter, the fact that it can transform matter and provide it with new borders, after having brought to it more expansion and fluidity, results from the surge and fire that desire includes.

Perhaps I could suggest that desire corresponds to a transcendental intuition in search of a truth which has a part of physical reality? And if desire succeeds in aspiring after a truth inscribed in nature or matter themselves, could a more suitable path towards the absolute exist? Then it is no longer a question of an absolute which can definitely reconcile subject with object, subject with predicate, but rather of an absolute which springs from a dynamic mediation between the subjective and the objective both in the self and between the selves.

Desire, the origin of which would be firstly light, would need the temperate fire of love to ensure such a mediation. Having faith in you would mean hoping that my intuition with regard to you could be fulfilled thanks to love, notably because it arose from a physical reality longing to become incarnate as truth: sexuate difference as the origin of my being. This difference is an original datum that not even scientists until now have succeeded in appropriating. If they can intervene in the somatic development of the embryo, they cannot create the germs or chromosomes which give birth to it. Their material existence and their dynamic potential are the source of our being in an irreducible way. And the desire between us is that which brings us back to this origin.

As well as in our origin as in our desire, matter and form cannot truly be distinguished from one another, either in each of the elements or in their union. Matter is already endowed with a structure which at once differentiates it and calls for a union with an other. And such an origin of our being is a real which potentially determines truth itself, ours and the one that we consider to be objective. This obvious fact has been unrecognized in our culture—hence, we lack a speech which contributes to developing more than destroying our living belonging and the most original and fruitful link between us.

Acknowledging this fact differs from our traditional understanding of truth itself. Now, the structure and the real—in a way the form and the content—do not separate from each other, which forces us to invent and put into practice another logic, in which truth does not divide from the real and from the dynamism of matter itself.

Henceforth, matter is no longer considered to be a product of consciousness, as is the case after Kant; it is taken to mean the living as such, what is more, the living animated by a consciousness belonging to the human being. And in order to last and to develop as living, human being cannot split up into subject and object, mind or idea and matter, unity and diversity. It is everything through its flesh, and it must discover how to cultivate the latter; that is to say, how to think of and incarnate itself in order to preserve this flesh from becoming an object, amongst others for the sciences, on the one hand, and, on the other hand, from becoming a source of energy for the functioning of technique or technologies—a logical abstraction only succeeding with difficulty in reunifying such a scission towards the absolute. Human being is then in exile with regard to its desire for the absolute, a desire that its own productions have removed from it.

The desire for the other, the relation of desire with a subject naturally different, is that which can give back its longing for the absolute to a human being by protecting it from being reduced to an object, and from being put in the neuter or subjected to structures or forms extraneous to the living being that it is.

In the relation of desire between two humans differently sexuated, it is a question of meeting between two subjective worlds. Even if each must resort to a subject–object logic, this must undergo a dialectical process in order that the meeting should take place. At this stage, each subjectivity remains dependent on a subject–object relation, above all subjective as far as it itself is concerned but objective for the other—to allude to the comments of Hegel (in *La différence entre les systèmes philosophiques de Fichte et de Schelling/The difference between Fichte's and Schelling's System of Philosophy*, 1986). This forces each to think about the nature of the subjective and the objective for itself and for the other in order to make possible a union in which longing for the absolute is preserved.

Such a longing for the absolute is as much, if not more, a desire to regain our flesh—that is, our physical matter already transformed by desire—and to transcend it, as to acquire a new shape or form. Indeed, if it were not the case, desire would above all aim at a repose. No doubt that the aspiration after a repose takes part in the desire for uniting with one another, but it cannot prevail over the force of attraction—for example, through a sort of regression to parental ties in which we still lack an autonomy and determination of our own, at least at a conscious level.

Such a relationship cannot correspond to the desire of an adult. The latter must assume, as much consciously as is possible, the particularity of each and transform an attraction, in which the force of gravity keeps a universal and undifferentiated character, apart from at a quantitative level, into a horizontal and qualitative attractiveness, which is wanted and in part gained with a view to a more spiritual becoming. Such a conversion can be achieved thanks to the longing between two humans who care about the accomplishment of their own being enough so as to work on their continuously being born or reborn here and now. Without contenting themselves with being merely subjected to gravity or denying its impact by resorting to supra-sensitive ideals, they search, through the levitation that desire can bring about, after another force that is of use for modifying the density of matter.

The disadvantage of a master–slave struggle in relation to that which the desire between us can provide is then understandable. Indeed, to what amounts the satisfaction of any possession in comparison with the ecstasy which can occur between two subjects in love with one another? But this asks for another way of conceiving of subjectivity, according to which our natural belonging is maintained, is acknowledged as determining and is transformed towards reaching an absolute which fits our desire. This desire now keeps an immediacy which feeds its energy, an immediacy which is no longer abstract and short in differentiation, but is specific and longs for combining with a differently determined immediacy.

Wanting to suppress the immediacy of the desire, merely our own or this for or of the other, in the name of a freedom in search of the absolute is thus a mistake. This amounts to destroying the energy necessary for such a quest, an energy more crucial than any satisfaction obtained through the mediation of an object, which anyway we will have to renounce and overcome. The matter is no longer one of destroying any object but of transforming our subjectivity itself, especially in order that it should become able to unite with another subjectivity, irreducibly external to our own. Indeed, this exteriority is crucial in our search for the absolute by supporting our desire, a desire which does not need any object to go from interiority to exteriority given its dealing with touch.

The Leading Part of Touch in Fleshly Dynamism

As Aristotle already points out in his *De Anima*, touch, differently from other senses, does not need mediation because it includes mediation in itself. And this mediation is able to evolve from a mere physical consistency to a more subtle energy. Touch, according to Aristotle, is always both matter and form and never exclusively one or the other. It can neither merge into matter without running the risk of vanishing nor become only form. It always comprises both and as such ensures a passage from our physical to our spiritual belonging, and this constantly. Touch is both substantial and in becoming. And its consistency as well as its evolution must maintain a measure which keeps it as a living touch, for oneself and also for the other.

Touch is an in-itself which is also a for-itself, but a for-itself which is both singular and common—a common which does not imply sameness but, nevertheless, allows a sharing to happen. What about this sharing? Most of the philosophers ignore such a question, whereas others openly assert the absence or their refusal of such a sharing—for example Jean-Paul Sartre, Maurice Merleau-Ponty and even Emmanuel Levinas in their discourses regarding the caress. Others—like Michel Henry—maintain that our inability to share touch is proved by the failure of our carnal union. What meaning can this union have for them? Is it not the place where it sometimes happens that the touching of the one and that of the other can end in a touching one another, and in a communion in which our physical matter becomes so subtle that it can reach the absolute while remaining matter?

Might I just as well say that the gravity and substance of our physical matter are then changed so that they should allow us to experience our flesh—and ourselves—as absolute? Does not the latter correspond to a transformation of matter which does not for all that dry up into mere form(s) but keeps a density which can lead us to an ecstasy thanks to its dynamic potential? This requires such a dynamism to differ from an attraction to, or by, emptiness, and correspond to a becoming more subtle of our flesh in order that we could live more fulfilled exchanges with the other.

Our physical matter, when it is livening up in this way, regains a dynamism which preserves it from a mere passivity, especially with regard to gravity. Nevertheless, it must keep a carnal density, though this has no longer the weight of a corpse: it is lighter and more porous—which permits it to retain cohesion and unity in its relation to and with the other. The structure that our sexuation provides, a structure which is turned both to the internal and the external of the organism, safeguards the possibility of experiencing our own flesh while opening it up to another flesh. In other words, I could say that placing myself in relation to the different living structure that the other represents is what allows each of us to protect our flesh from vanishing into the abstract universality of the human species.

Our sexuate structure brings together unity, consistency and limits to the living being that we are. It provides us with the physical resistance of a specific structure, and also with the spiritual dynamism of the desire that arises from between the two, which enables us to become aware of our sexuate belonging. And a meeting between two fleshes cannot end in removing one of the two, or reducing one to a mere plastic or elastic consistency which leaves its own space to the other. Instead, meeting needs a transformation of each towards a communion which does not destroy the duality of carnal subjectivities.

Such an ability to modify the physical nature of matter thanks to a carnal communion is perhaps specific to humanity, at least as a path towards a spiritual becoming and not only towards copulation or reproduction. Rather, it then mainly aims to lead the human being to accomplish what or who it is without going no further than only reproducing, either oneself or another human. To succeed in this evolution, we have to overcome categories in use until now, in particular oppositions such as internal–external, corporal–incorporeal, matter–spirit. Emphasizing quality and difference is one of the means to carry out such an undertaking, especially through resorting to another economy than the traditional one regarding the relations between matter and form.

Remaining in an economy governed by similarity, I perceive my genus only as the same as the other, thus not as different, apart from as opposite. If qualities are considered to be specific to my genus and in a way which brings a content to it, notably thanks to the unity through which it puts them together even though they determine it, then things happen otherwise. By my belonging to a genus, I correspond with a world which is different from, but not opposite to, the one of the other genus. As such these worlds can approach and fertilize one another, provided that each takes on the particularity of its genus and the partiality that it represents in relation to a universality which would be merely spiritual and supposedly in the neuter.

Qualities are capable of going from the outside to the inside of the body, and they are not necessarily subjected to gravity. Moreover, they are their densities—which does not mean their weights, their contrasts, their forces of attraction, and so on—which contribute towards putting in touch and even uniting two different worlds without for all that dismantling the structure of one or the other.

Qualities have also the ability to link together the corporal with the spiritual, especially because they create an inner physical place which can address our spirit. They allow us to identify the other at the carnal level too. Qualities are able to build, in us and between us, bridges and mediations between matter and spirit. And, if they can stimulate our needs—for example, the one of eating—the latter cannot abolish them. They subsist as a beyond that needs cannot destroy by their satisfaction. Could I say that they subsist as an element of desire—a desire in which matter and form are indissociable from and irreducible to one another? Hence a constant opening up to the infinite, but also a relation to touch under different modalities.

Touch, indeed, is not perceptible without being together matter and form. But it is then a question of a form which is drawn into flesh itself and which is experienced more than it is seen. This probably explains why the potential of our touch has been unrecognized by a culture which favours sight, outside, seizure, nerves linked with muscles to the detriment of touch, sky and mucous, intimacy, elusiveness and flesh as a sensitive medium.

For lack of attention, cultivation and even perception regarding it, touch vanishes into an external and undifferentiated empathy scarcely conscious as well of oneself as of the other; which transforms our flesh into a sort of almost inanimate and opaque corporeal matter. The ability of flesh to know, remember, change, evolve and share is then neglected. This deprives us of a crucial potential for our human becoming and keeps us divided into body and spirit, lacking a flesh capable of acting as a mediation, especially between us as two different beings.

By adhering to the external world or remaining trapped within it, we have not become able to build the world which corresponds with us, a world of which any living being is badly in need, and in which the little child seems to still live, but that our culture forces us to leave. Hence, we wander in search of ourselves, of the other, of a habitable world. We survive, borrowing from matter, culture and the other(s), without really caring about how to develop ourselves as living beings, and even unable to still perceive that which our being consists in, its desire(s) and its becoming.

Loss of Differentiation Due to Sight

Our lack of differentiation from the world paradoxically results from the prerogative that our culture attaches to sight. We end in making one with what we see, as Merleau-Ponty asserts. The sense which underlies our theory, more generally our culture, is a sense which brings about our mistaking the one who perceives for what is perceived. Hence a logic which focuses on adequacy in the subject–object relation. Then, the subject–subject relationship is not yet possible, each subjectivity being immersed in a universe of objects from which it cannot truly distinguish itself.

Carrying out a reversal of the hierarchy between the senses is necessary in order that the subject could emerge as such from the background. It is touch which will allow our subjectivity to gain this individuation, and in particular a touching or retouching oneself which can be at the origin of a differentiated self-consciousness. Sight, which is presumed to be the sense of discrimination, is finally what immerses us in the world in which we are, whereas touch allows us to become an autonomous living being and to live in our own world.

The world that we must first inhabit is the one of our living body, of our flesh, and not a world built and told, one way or another, by the logos. We must succeed in saying ourselves in order that we could place ourselves in the saying of the world in which we live. And we must embody our difference before subjecting our existence to systems of equivalences which structure the logos and the world. The saying of nature in us ought to be capable of assessing the symbolic order that the surrounding world imposes on us.

It is not the prerogative of sight which permits the saying of our nature to be expressed. Instead, it is this way fragmented and objectified, unless to be reduced to a projection onto the beyond or the future, from which some images, reflections and even speculations sometimes are sent back to us. So, we are deprived of the perception of our natural belonging. And the tactile experience, which more truly tells this belonging, more often than not vanishes into the visual universe in which we are exiled. If an individuation of our bodies, and thus their distinction from the world and from the others, occurs in such a universe, it is no longer a question of autonomous living beings which enter into relations through a dynamism which is their own. Henceforth, we are dealing with an artificially fabricated world, a world without differentiation, distance and freedom—a world extraneous to life. And the assimilation—the 'colonization', according to Merleau-Ponty— of touch by sight makes impossible the tactile experience thanks to which we could recover for ourselves, and also return to the other(s), a threshold which both allows us to gather with ourselves and the others to gather with themselves as the living organisms that we are, and also to open up to the other(s) and to the world.

Such a gathering and an opening-up are neither in the neuter nor lacking in differentiation: from the beginning they are sexuate. Considering this sexuation to be only a stage—for example, an oral or anal pregenital stage—prior to sexual intercourse strictly speaking amounts to denying or unrecognizing that our experience of ourselves, of the world and of the other is at once comprehensively sexuate. Indeed, an energy and a desire which correspond with our sexuate belonging animates us from our birth, and in a way from our conception.

Sexuate difference in the manner of perceiving ourselves, the world and the other(s) is then a qualitative difference, which will be later reduced to a quantitative one. And yet, quality belongs to another experience than that which has been favoured by our culture. Such an experience requires us to listen to and accept passively in ourselves what happens and be able to transform it into other than an immediate external activity. It needs the cultivation of an internal touch as the elaboration of an intimate space extraneous to the opacity of matter. It is not only through our sight that we can perceive the world and the other(s), by means of images or representations, it is also through the trace in ourselves of their way of touching us. Such a perception is less momentary, fragmentary and external than the visual perception, and it is more easily integrated into an organic living totality than into a totality mentally constructed.

At least it can go in this way if we take time to linger on such a perception, instead of merely assimilating and incorporating it into what or who we already are. It is also possible if we consider it to be a potential factor of our development and that of the between us—which compels us to adopt another manner of experiencing space and time, and to live what happens in ourselves beyond the alternative introjection-rejection, with which many philosophers content themselves. In order that what touches us and tells us in the intimacy of our flesh might take shape, another manner of thinking is needed, one which considers the truth of sensitivity itself. This requires us to be able to differ from the other(s) by and for ourselves, a possibility that belonging to a genus can grant us without the length that other processes of individuation necessitate— for example, the evolution of human spin, brain or hand.

Such a process of individuation cannot be achieved by denying the by-itself and for-itself of the other. I must acknowledge that the other is capable of a for-itself, with which it can provide itself—which asks me to take on a negative not with respect to the other but with respect to the particularity of the by-myself and for-myself and my longing for the infinite and the absolute. From such a perspective it is acceptable to suggest that, in our culture, until now the man has imposed his by-himself and for-himself as universally valid without acknowledging the viewpoint of the other as different.

Acknowledging the potential reality and truth of the by-itself and for-itself of the other as different is a stage of individuation that humanity has not yet reached. And yet, this stage is crucial for us connecting truth with ethics. Indeed, to gain our individuation as belonging to a specific genus entails defining a place in which to dwell, a dwelling in ourselves, that we must respect and which must determine our way of entering into relations with ourselves, with the world and with the other(s).

This place is our own, but the other can be present in it, both externally and internally. The other does not amount to what we too often reduce it: an object that we can appropriate or an embodiment of the negative against which we can pit ourselves. The other is an element of the environment in which I live and of the nature that I, myself, am and with which I must negotiate for being and becoming the one who I am.

The other corresponds with an aspiration which lies in me but I cannot appropriate—as I can in a way do with regard to my needs.

Unless I understand my need for the other to be due to the fact that this other can resist being shaped, assimilated or destroyed by me in what is particular to it. My want of the other exceeds my singularity while preserving it. It is a call for a beyond, for an infinite which does not abolish me but answers an intimate aspiration in search of its fulfilment. It represents the need for a transcendence in order to achieve my becoming. As such, my want of the other cannot be satisfied—at once it is longing for a beyond, an absolute, and even a universal after which aspiring constitutes me as a human subject. The need for the other as other in reality is desire. And it is between two different desires that the universal, the absolute, the infinite can happen without being ever appropriated by either of them.

Desire unites in an individual spirit with the body. Through its gravity a body is already individualized with respect to the universe in which it takes place, but through desire it can appropriate this weight as its own and modify it. Indeed, the gravitation that my body undergoes is both specific and non-appropriable; it is an objectivity which is imposed on my subjectivity. However, thanks to desire, the latter can act on gravity, but the becoming lighter that desire can grant is truly physical or merely ideal. Indeed, a subjection to supra-sensitive ideas or ideals can provoke a sort of weightlessness, but this more often than not has nothing to do with my body and can even make me experience it as heavier.

The desire for and of the other, and above all a shared desire, is able to give rise to a phenomenon of levitation which transforms the weight of the body itself. It takes part in our individuation, both in an active and a passive way, through its impact on the density and the cohesion of our flesh. Sexual desire, even any sexuate desire, above all can contribute towards such a transformation, and it is an aspect of our nature on which subjectivity can act so as to modify our physical gravity and make it more compatible with a spiritual experience. It is a means of overcoming the opposition between body and spirit and also of changing our relation to gravity in order to harmonize it with that of the other.

Living Individuation Shaped by Mutual Desire

We have to keep a unity in order to preserve our desire for the absolute. We must experience ourselves as a whole, not only the merely organic whole of our natural belonging but the whole that we acquire thanks to desire. It is desire which grants us an experience of the infinite which is not merely that of life but which corresponds with our wish to reach the absolute. We are those, as determined subjectivities, who can safeguard our relation to the absolute, and not only life as such. And it is our sexuation, as a structure which can unify the multitude of our sensitive experiences, which can provide us with the immanence of a whole destined to transcend itself.

When we are exiled from such a whole, we are also exiled from our longing for the absolute, deprived of the relation to the simplicity that it represents and which is able to transform multiplicity into infinity. Keeping our desire alive amounts to maintaining a passage from a natural absolute to a spiritual absolute. It contributes to preserving our longing for the infinite not only as a driving surge towards becoming ourselves but also as a motion towards uniting with the other in order to become the ones who we are.

Cultivating our desire is also a means to ensure the connection between freedom and limits. These are no longer imposed from an outside as a restriction or an opposition to the exercise of our freedom. They belong to our being itself and represent a structure outside of which it cannot unfold endlessly towards its accomplishment. Sexuation is not external to us but is a living structure starting from which we can develop.

Sexuation requires a dialectical process between my becoming as sexuate and my relation to and with an other differently sexuated. The motion corresponding to such dialectics is other than the one at work in the Hegelian dialectics. Indeed, the other sex is not opposite to mine: it is both same and different. We have no longer a word to express such a meaning that the Greek *heteros* still conveyed. The other sex—as the other hand, the other foot, the other lip, the other eye—signifies an other of two, whose individuation and relationship involves a really specific economy. The same as and different from the other, each element of the pair has an autonomy that is granted it notably through its relation to the other. Entering into relation with one another takes place through a finite structure which appears, is cleared, thanks to the space that, then, exists between the two.

Gaining our individuation implies that we maintain such a space, thus that we renounce the immediacy of a fulfilled union with the other. This asks for a certain heroism from us given the longing for uniting with one another which supports the dynamism of our desire. It is no longer through conflicts and wars, as it is from a Hegelian perspective, or by opposing the other that individuation is gained; rather, it is by preserving our difference and thanks to the restraint that this needs. Each must thus dwell in itself, keeping its desire as particular, without it merely merging or being confused with the desire of the other. Holding back from fulfilling the immediacy of our surges in order to respect the other transforms the nature of our desire, raises it to a transcendental level where the for-ourselves becomes a possible for-the-other.

Such a process is without end, it is never achieved once and for all and it requires us to be as much vigilant as wide awake. It results from taking into account a determination which grants us a margin of freedom with respect to our physical materiality and our needs in general, something that our belonging to a people cannot guarantee to us. Hence the necessity of waging war, according to Hegel? Our sexuation gets, for us, the possibility of remaining within ourselves on the condition that we constantly expose ourselves to open up to, and even to unite with, the other. It gives us a freedom which involves our being able to keep ourselves independent and autonomous whatever our longing for becoming the other or for losing our individuation in uniting with the other.

This does not occur without courage, but a courage different from the one which is needed for waging war. However, if Hegel considers the man capable of being courageous during war to be free, a war which answers a spiritual requirement according to him, the man capable of being courageous in love would show higher courage, freedom and spirituality. Instead of expecting from war a sort of negation of negation, man, then and in my opinion, takes on an insurmountable negative, and in this way works continually on the transformation of spirit itself. Man no longer entrusts the safeguard of spirit to a people or a state, a process through which spirit becomes paralyzed by being frozen in fixed values, and thus needs conflicts in order to be set in motion again. Indeed, desire has lost its dynamism; it has become dependent on values presumed to be ideal but which are acknowledged as such only by a given community at a given moment of history and according to the place where this community takes place.

Because of the static character of such values, the connection between nature and culture gets lost and disappears, a link that only desire can continuously ensure in the present on the condition that it succeeds in freeing itself from what is already established by a people, notably through its history. By considering that a people corresponds to the incarnation of the individual, Hegel underestimates the necessary mediation of desire for the individual and the collective becomings. He does not take into account sufficiently the living way through which each can and must contribute towards forming the whole that it itself is and connecting it to a community. Hence, it is with death, more than with life, than humanity is confronted, and heroism consists less in making life blossom than in risking it for a people through war.

By alienating the dynamism of desire in the life of a people without having first cultivated it in the relationships with the naturally different other(s), the citizens, as they are imagined by Hegel, miss the necessary connection and constant interaction between nature and culture and the work of the negative that they imply. From this results the Hegelian search for creating a motion inside of a world cut off from its natural energy resources, a motion which will be kept going by confronting oppositions, which artificially and inadequately substitute for a natural energy. Conflicts and wars then represent processes which aim at arousing again an energy which, in reality, they instead exhaust.

6

Provisory Synthesis: Difference Can Overcome Contradiction

If some philosophers have claimed that our own 'to be', as the one of other living beings, corresponds to a will, then they have not really questioned the nature of this will. And they have subjected it to reason without realizing the consequences of this gesture. This is particularly true with regard to Hegel.

And yet, it is possible to interrogate our will—our appetite, our aspiration, our desire—as that which takes over from the moving by itself that Aristotle defines as the characteristic of a living being. Human beings cannot develop only from the origin of their life. This origin does not belong to them because they were born from the conjunction of two human beings, what is more two who are different by nature. This origin is also stolen from them because of their original immaturity and their consequent dependence on others for satisfying their needs. Their will is that which remains of a motion of growing after they reached their physical maturity. But this will has not to be reduced to a mere will of reason, instead of being acknowledged as a will relating to our whole being. Which of the philosophers has taken a real interest in this aspect of our will and in a way that would allow it to become incarnate and blossom? And who has really wondered about a reason suitable for a

© The Author(s) 2019
L. Irigaray, *Sharing the Fire*,
https://doi.org/10.1007/978-3-030-28330-8_6

cultivation of our will to be, instead of subjecting it to the rule of reason itself?

However, the fact that our culture does not support our will to continue growing through our desire keeps alive the resentment that Nietzsche considers to be characteristic of our tradition. Nietzsche speaks of resentment as a sentiment that we experience against the time which passes. Could I suggest that this resentment results from the fact that time passes without we ourselves becoming? Our philosophy made our becoming dependent on timeless ideas or ideals instead of proposing cultural means which could accompany and favour our growing as living beings. Acting in this way, it aroused resentment through paralyzing our will to grow—which amounts to paralyzing our will to live.

Our being as living wants us to become. And the passing character that becoming involves is an expression of our living belonging, to which we are faithful by growing more than by not being. Resentment, even desire for revenge, which prevent us from becoming the new human that we have to be, are the outcome of our incapacity for making blossom our 'to be' as living. And is not the solution that Nietzsche suggests in order to overcome resentment a manner of freezing the problem? Does not the eternal return of the same take away from time its remainder of life? Does not the true overcoming of nihilism require another way of conceiving of temporality—one which allows our becoming to unfold through a transformation of the past into the future? Is not our resentment against the time which passes an outcome of the dissociation of temporality from our natural growing, a dissociation that Nietzsche seems in a way to increase more than reduce? How can we become as living beings if temporality amounts to an eternal return of the same? And how could we govern the world without taking into account its and our both natural and cultural evolution? Does not overcoming resentment instead ask us to inhabit time so that it should be the place which permits a continuity in becoming—our own, that of the world and of our relationship with the other, with others?

Time must be a sort of living dwelling which accompanies our becoming. And the same goes for time as for our natural belonging: it needs to be cultivated in order that life should be able to grow, to blossom, to flower and to bear fruit. Indeed, making our becoming continuous does not occur without assuming an original discontinu-ity—with regard to our origin, but also to the living beings different from ourselves. We have to take on the particularity of our own being and that of the temporality suitable for it, but this temporality cannot cut us off from life, as our culture generally did. We must succeed in cultivating life so that we could remain living without being immersed in a flow which lacks differentiation and individuation. This requires us to be faithful to nature without either subjecting it or being subjected to it. Hence the need for us to overcome a first immediacy in our relat-ing to nature and its temporality while ensuring a continuity to it—which necessitates another dialectics than the speculative dialectics of Hegel. We no longer have the power to handle by ourselves the nega-tive in order to reach an objective absolute which corresponds with our subjectivity. We have to take on the non-being which is from the very beginning our destiny as particular beings.

Starting from such an assumption, we differently perceive the nature of being. We are even attracted by the being which appeals to us by its absence or withdrawal from us, a being the removal of which summons us and after which we aspire. And the matter, henceforth, is no longer one of discovering and showing a being hidden from us in this way, but of uniting with it, without for all that appropriating it. The ques-tion is no longer one of perceiving only through spirit either, of being concerned or engaged only with our consciousness in order to unveil something of being, but of also agreeing to be affected and to venture to be touched, even to abandon ourselves to this affection, in order to allow our 'to be' to happen in a way that remains hidden from our sight. We can only make ourselves available in order that this 'to be' should occur without any seizure on our part.

Wanting to institute a dialectics of sensitivity with our traditional mode of thinking proves thus to be impossible. Indeed, representation, evalua-tion through a merely intellectual judgement, logic favouring the subject–object(s) relations have been imagined and used from its misapplication, not to say its repression. Contrasting poetry with thought does not solve the problem either. Rather, the matter is one of wondering about what was at stake in our way of thinking and how we can modify it. We must think about what our traditional discourse, about what the logos, is able to say and what it maintains outside its saying, either because it does not aim to tell it or because its way of saying prevents it from perceiving and expressing this non-said. In other words we must wonder about what absence or withdrawal of meaning goes with that which we consider to be the rational way of saying the real and of sharing it.

The real which seems to have been dismissed by our cultural tradition is the one which relates to desire and fire, desire as fire. This crucial aspect of our existence seems to have been neglected by philosophy and left to religion, especially for a sacrificial use, and this from the archaic traditions. The most ancient versions of the Vedas tell that originally fire ought to have been the property of the original waters, sometimes named Mothers, which, by their becoming heated, would have produced the cosmic egg from which the world would have sprung. The god Agni, first born of the ardour of the original waters, would have stolen the fire from the maternal-feminine world to give it to the warlike masculine gods, in particular to the god Indra, who this way would have subjected or won over the feminine original potential. To organize or build what had been generated by the original waters was, then, the role of men. One of their main deeds was to lay out the sacrificial era as a place where the perpetuation of the cosmic order was cared for. The responsibility for the sacrificial rites was entrusted to Agni, as the god of fire, after he had betrayed his own maternal ascendance to swear allegiance to the clan of Indra in exchange for immortality.

The fire seems to have never been shared. After having been a generative potential of the elements, sometimes called Mothers, it has been stolen by men, thanks to their warlike masculine gods, and put at the service of their work of fabrication of a more or less artificial world. It also has been of use to men for making sacrifices to the gods, notably because they felt guilty about having appropriated the fire.

Fire has never been preserved and cultivated through sharing a mutual desire, beginning with a sexuate desire—preservation and cultivation which in a way correspond with those of a non-being. The origin of being, notably through its potential for uniting, the fire arising from our sexuate belonging is nothing by itself. It remains extraneous to what characterizes being in our tradition. Its main property is to unite, but uniting acts without producing itself as being. It happens without appearing, without a specific presence of what unites. The latter does not enter into presence, it is never positioned before the subject, never visible. It operates while holding itself back. It intervenes, in particular between two, without belonging to the one or to the other. It is—but the properties of this 'to be' are not those that we traditionally attribute to being and its truth. Its mode of acting is without presence, permanency, even consistency. Nevertheless, it is—both not nothing and not being. And assuming this not being is the condition of its existence, of its being not nothing. It overcomes the dichotomy of being/not being, happening before or beyond such a split.

The fire of our sexuate desire acts as a verb which operates before the final and permanent determination of the substantives that it connects. Indeed, it unites each with itself and with the other(s). It gathers what or who already existed, without truly being by themselves, both within their selves and between their selves. Differently from the logos, which gathers elements which are by themselves and need to be committed to memory and assembled, the fire awoken by our sexuate desire gives meaning to elements by putting them together, by joining them to one another. But this link corresponds to what gives sense to them without bending them to another sense than their own. Indeed, the latter calls for uniting with one another.

Meaning then is the union itself, a union which is both a finality and a means on the condition that we agree that these escape from our mastery. We must answer for our 'to be' without being truly capable of making it exist. We can only pave the way to its happening by being faithful to our natural belonging, by listening to its call for uniting with the other, and by letting occur what results from uniting with one another as naturally and transcendentally different. This requires us to renounce appropriating that for which we long.

Without any aim that we could appropriate, our desire is not without truth. Alas, we use the source and the framework—in a way the *Gestell*—of our most original desire for producing other than truth. We have not really wondered about the truth of our desire as sexuate. We have just transformed our sexuate belonging into a device for producing something. We have made it an instrument of exploitation more than a means of unveiling our truth and cultivating it. We have not acknowledged the transcendental resource and quality of our sexuate belonging. We have used our sexuation to return to a mere ontical destiny, what is more in a frequently destructive manner, without considering its ontological potential. And yet, the latter is crucial for our blossoming as humans, although it is really particular and eludes our usual way of conceiving of our destiny. Desire exists, but we cannot seize it in any way.

Desire operates our gathering ourselves together and our gathering with one another. It prompts our opening and closing up, our blossoming and withdrawing, our becoming and our faithfulness to ourselves. Sexuate desire compels us to abandon ourselves to the other while so revealing to ourselves who we are. Nothing is more dialectical by itself than sexuate desire, but it escapes from any rational domination. We must assume our not being the other without any mastery of this nothingness, if not taking it on as an unsurmountable negative. This assent, one could also say this assumption, allows desire to exist, but this existence remains without being of its own. It corresponds to an aspiration after that which is non-appropriable by anyone—a pure link between us, between all.

Returning to desire its nature—in a way its essence, this term having now a new meaning—extraneous to any appropriable being, we return to ourselves, and also to the word, our destiny. We discover that, as well as desire, our words must serve to unite living beings in the respect for our/their difference(s). To be a human would correspond to be the guardian of a fire which does not consume but gives birth, gives life to each other. A destiny that, I hope, could suit all sorts of divinities.

Selected Bibliography

Aristotle. 1980. *De l'âme*, texte établi par A. Jannone, traduit et annoté par E. Barbotin. Paris: Les Belles Lettres [*De Anima*, translated by Mark Shiffman. Indianapolis and Cambridge: Hackett, 2011].

Clerc, Roger. 1979. *Manuel de Yoga*. Paris: Le Courrier du Livre.

Hegel, Georg Wilhelm Friedrich. 1966. *La Phénoménologie de l'Esprit, Tomes I et II*, traduit par Jean Hyppolite. Paris: Editions Aubier-Montaigne [*Phenomenology of Spirit*, translated by A.V. Miller, edited by J.N. Findlay. Oxford: Oxford University Press, 1979].

Hegel, Georg Wilhelm Friedrich. 1970. *Encyclopédie des Sciences philosophiques en abrégé*, traduit par Maurice de Gandillac. Paris: NRF/Gallimard [*Georg Wilhelm Friedrich Hegel: Encyclopaedia of the Philosophical Sciences in Basic Outline*, translated and edited by Klaus Brinkmann and Daniel O. Dahlstrom. Cambridge: Cambridge University Press, 2010].

Hegel, Georg Wilhelm Friedrich. 1972. *Le droit naturel*. Traduit et préfacé par Albert Kaan. Paris: NRF/Gallimard [*Natural Law*, translated by T.M. Knox. Philadelphia: University of Pennsylvania Press, 1975].

Hegel, Georg Wilhelm Friedrich. 1986. *La différence entre les systèmes philosophiques de Fichte et de Schelling*, traduit par Bernard Gilson. Paris: Vrin [*The Difference between Fichte's and Schelling's System of Philosophy*, translated and edited by H.S. Harris and Walter Cerf. Albany: State University of New York Press, 1977].

Heidegger, Martin. 1958a. 'La question de la technique', dans *Essais et Conférences*, traduit par André Préau, 9–48. Paris: Gallimard ['The Question Concerning Technology', in *The Question Concerning Technology and Other Essays*, translated by William Lovitt, 3–35. New York: Harper and Row, 1977].

Heidegger, Martin. 1958b. 'La chose' dans *Essais et Conférences*, traduit par André Préau, 194–218. Paris: Editions Gallimard ['The Thing,' in *Poetry, Language, Thought*, translated by Albert Hofstadter, 163–180. New York: Harper Collins, 1971].

Heidegger, Martin. 1958c. 'Bâtir, Habiter, Penser', dans *Essais et conférences*, traduit par André Préau, 170–193. Paris: Les Essais/Gallimard.

Heidegger, Martin. 1964. *L'Être et le Temps*, traduit par Rudolph Boehm et Alphonse De Waelhens. Paris: NRF/Gallimard [*Being and Time*, translated by John Macquarrie and Edward Robinson. Oxford: Blackwell Publishers, 1962].

Heidegger, Martin. 1967a. 'Sur la grammaire et l'étymologie du mot "être"', dans *Introduction à la métaphysique*, traduit par Albert Kahn, 80–83. Paris: Gallimard [*Introduction to Metaphysics*, translated by Gregory Fried and Richard Polt, 74–78. New Haven: Yale University Press, 2000].

Heidegger, Martin. 1967b. *Qu'appelle-t-on penser?* traduit par Aloys Becker et Gérard Granel. Paris: Presses Universitaires de France [*What Is Called Thinking?* translated by Fred D. Wieck and J. Glenn Gray. New York and London: Harper and Row, 1968].

Heidegger, Martin. 1976. 'Temps et être, Protocole d'un séminaire sur la conference "Temps et être"' dans *Questions IV*, traduit par Jean Beaufret, François Fédier, Jean Lauxerois et Claire Roë, 11–106. Paris: NRF/Gallimard ['Time and Being' and 'Summary of a Seminar on the Lecture«Time and Being»', in *On Time and Being*, translated by Joan Stambaugh, 1–55. Chicago: University of Chicago Press, 2002].

Heidegger, Martin. 1993. 'Building, Dwelling, Thinking', in *Basic Writings: From Being and Time (1927) to The Task of Thinking (1964)*, edited by David Farrell Krell, 343–363. London and New York: Routledge.

Henry, Michel. 2000. *Incarnation: Une philosophie de la chair*. Paris, Editions du Seuil [*Incarnation: A Philosophy of Flesh*, translated by Karl Hefty. Evanston: Northwestern University Press, 2015].

Husserl, Edmond. 1982. *Recherches phénoménologiques pour la constitution*. Paris, Puf, traduit par Eliane Escouba.

Hyppolite, Jean. 1983. *Introduction à la philosophie de l'Histoire de Hegel.* Paris: Editions du Seuil.

Irigaray, Luce. 1974. *Speculum.* Paris, Editions de Minuit [*Speculum*, translated by Gilliam C. Gill. Ithaca, NY: Cornell University Press, 1985].

Irigaray, Luce. 1987. *Sexes et parentés* Paris. Editions de Minuit [*Sexes and Genealogies*, translated by Gillian C. Gill. New York: Columbia University Press, 1993].

Irigaray, Luce. 1993. *J'aime à toi. Esquisse d'une félicité dans l'Histoire.* Paris: Grasset [*I Love to You: Sketch for a Felicity within History*, translated by Alison Martin. New York and London: Routledge, 1996].

Irigaray, Luce. 2017. *To Be Born.* London: Palgrave Macmillan.

Les Yogasutras de Patanjali. 1979. Commentés par Swâmi Sanânda Sarasvati Paris, Le courrier du livre [*Yogânusânam*, Swami Sananda Sarasvati. Harlem, 'Yoga-Vedanta Mandir', 1976].

Levinas, Emmanuel. 1961. *Totalité et Infini: Essai sur l'extériorité.* La Haye: Martinus Nijhoff [*Totality and Infinity: An Essay on Exteriority*, translated by Alphonso Lingis. Dordrecht: Kluwer Academic, 1991].

Levinas, Emmanuel. 1979. *Le temps et l'autre.* Montpelier: Fata Morgana [*Time and the Other, and Additional Essays*, translated by Richard A. Cohen. Pittsburgh: Duquesne University Press, 1987].

Merleau-Ponty, Maurice. 1984 [1964]. *Le visible et l'invisible.* Paris: NRF/Gallimard [*The Visible and the Invisible*, translated by Alphonso Lingis. Evanston: Northwestern University Press, 1968].

Merleau-Ponty, Maurice. 1995. *Nature, Notes du cours au Collège de France.* Paris: Editions du Seuil [*Nature: Course Notes from the College de France*, translated by Robert Vallier. Evanston: Northwestern University Press, 2003].

Nietzsche, Friedrich. 1971. *Ainsi parlait Zarathoustra*, traduit par Maurice de Gandillac. Paris: NRF/Gallimard [*Thus Spoke Zarathustra,* translated By Graham Parkes. Oxford: Oxford University Press, 2005].

Sartre, Jean Paul. 1943–1970. *L'être et le néant.* Paris: NRF/Gallimard [*Being and Nothingness; An Essay in Phenomenological Ontology*, translated by Hazel E. Barnes. New York: Citadel Press, 2001].

Schelling, F. W. J. ou Hegel, G. W. F. 1986. 'De la relation entre la philosophie de la nature et la philosophie en général', dans *La différence entre les systèmes philosophiques de Fichte et de Schelling*, traduit par Bernard Gilson, 201–218.

Printed by Printforce, the Netherlands